Dimensions of Moral Theory

M000313841

Dimensions of Moral Theory

An Introduction to Metaethics and Moral Psychology

JONATHAN JACOBS

Blackwell
Publishing

BLACKWELL PUBLISHING
350 Main Street, Malden, MA 02148-5020, USA
9600 Garsington Road, Oxford OX4 2DQ, UK
550 Swanston Street, Carlton, Victoria 3053, Australia

First published 2002 by Blackwell Publishing Ltd

2   2006

Library of Congress Cataloging-in-Publication Data

Jacobs, Jonathan A.
    Dimensions of moral theory : an introduction to metaethics and moral psychology /
Jonathan Jacobs.
        p. cm.
    Includes bibliographical references and index.
    ISBN 0-631-22963-9 (alk. paper) — ISBN 0-631-22964-7 (pbk. : alk. paper)
    1. Ethics.   2. Psychology and philosophy.   I. Title.

BJ1012 .J295 2002
170'.42—dc21

                                                              2002066434

ISBN-13: 978-0-631-22963-6 (alk. paper) — ISBN-13: 978-0-631-22964-3 (pbk. : alk. paper)

A catalogue record for this title is available from the British Library.

Set in 11 on 13pt Baskerville
by Ace Filmsetting Ltd, Frome, Somerset

The publisher's policy is to use permanent paper from mills that operate a sustainable
forestry policy, and which has been manufactured from pulp processed using acid-free and
elementary chlorine-free practices. Furthermore, the publisher ensures that the text paper
and cover board used have met acceptable environmental accreditation standards.

For further information on
Blackwell Publishing, visit our website:
www.blackwellpublishing.com

Contents

Preface

Moral theories address questions about what is right and wrong, what is obligatory, what is impermissible, what our ideals should be, and the like. This book examines the key presuppositions and philosophical commitments that support and shape moral theories. Many of the topics discussed belong to what is called "metaethics," which is a study of moral concepts, language, and thought, rather than a study of moral issues themselves. Other topics in the book come under the heading of "moral psychology" and concern fundamental issues about the nature of moral agents, moral motivation, and the roles of reason, desire, and pleasure in moral action and experience. *Dimensions of Moral Theory* is not meant to be a comprehensive survey of metaethical and moral psychological positions and arguments. It is intended to introduce you to the issues and to show how they are generated and why they are important. It thereby brings to light some of the most important philosophical problems raised by moral theorizing.

Any moral theory, whatever its specific content, will presuppose a stand concerning the nature of moral value, the character of moral motivation, and the status of moral judgments. For example, we can ask whether moral judgments are assertions that are literally true or false. Or are they expressions of attitudes or feelings? (Asserting a fact is quite different from expressing a feeling.) Is moral value an objective reality that exists independently of our concerns, interests, and feelings, or is it somehow dependent upon or reflective of them? When we are motivated to act on moral considerations is that because we recognize that moral behavior is rationally required, or because we have certain feelings, or because it is in our self-interest? When we reason about the morally relevant features of actions should we be thinking primarily in terms of consequences, motives, or something else? These are the sorts of questions discussed in *Dimensions of Moral Theory*. They are questions *about* moral thought and judgment and moral value, rather than questions within moral theorizing about what we should do or how we should live.

When you study a moral theory you probably will not find a sentence in it that reads: "Moral value is objective in the following sense," followed by an account of the objectivity of value. There may not be a sentence that reads, "Moral claims cannot assert moral facts, because there are none and thus, moral claims are not literally true or false." Still, commitments concerning the status of moral value and moral claims are part of the essential architecture of a theory. The same is true with respect to matters such as the relation of reason and desire, and the relation between moral value and non-moral facts. Those commitments reflect the theorist's position on the philosophically most fundamental features of morality and they do a great deal of the work. This book will help you identify and critically examine those philosophical commitments and arguments.

There are four chapters and each takes up some central concern of theorizing about morality, shows what motivates that concern, and shows what is at stake in addressing it in different ways. A view about any one of the issues will often make a difference to how the others are viewed. For that reason, the book also makes connections between the discussions in each chapter so that you can see how these fundamental concerns bear on each other. Indeed, that is part of what is exciting about studying philosophy; namely, the ways in which seemingly unrelated issues have important implications for each other.

Chapter 1 is a discussion of the status of moral value. By "status" I mean the issue of whether moral value is objective (and if so, in what sense) or subjective (and if so, in what sense). Suppose moral values are objective. Is that exactly the same kind of objectivity as scientific objectivity? If moral values are subjective, are they subjective in the same ways that matters of taste are subjective, or that aesthetic values are (if *they* are subjective)? What would lead a theorist to maintain a specific view on the question of objectivity and subjectivity? How do those commitments help us understand moral thought and judgments? Are we to regard moral claims as being literally true or false, correct or mistaken, or is there some other measure by which they are evaluated?

If moral values are subjective does that in any way undermine the authority of moral considerations or weaken their claim on us?

Chapter 2 examines issues of what is broadly called "moral psychology." It comprises questions about moral motivation, the moral significance of pleasure and happiness, the role of self-interest in morality, and a set of problems concerning what is called "moral luck." In discussing moral luck we are talking about the ways in which moral value and the moral evaluation of acts and agents depend upon features that we, as agents, cannot directly or fully control. Some of the questions about moral luck are already familiar to us in our reflections about how to morally judge well intentioned acts that have untoward consequences, or acts with objectionable motives that nonetheless do good, and so forth. The topics discussed in this chapter all arise in natural and related ways in reflecting on morality and moral theory. Are all actions, including moral actions, really self-interested? Can an agent be immoral without being irrational? Is reason or desire or feeling the basis of moral concern and motivation? Issues of moral psychology are just as important as questions about moral value. Indeed, metaethics and moral psychology jointly constitute much of the philosophical infrastructure of moral theorizing.

With the resources of chapters 1 and 2 we will be in a position to examine some of the main strategies of moral theorizing in chapter 3. There are different approaches to structuring moral theory, based on different conceptions of what has moral value. Is moral value found in motives, or in the outcomes of actions, or in the principles upon which agents act, or in agents' characters, or something else, or some combination of these? The overall approach of a theory will depend upon what it is that the theory claims morally *matters*. A theory in which actions are held to be intrinsically right or wrong will have a different structure from a theory according to which moral value is in the consequences of actions. This issue of the "location" of moral value is already familiar to us. We all struggle with difficult questions about the moral weight of motives, outcomes, and agents' characters. Is one of those *the* source of moral value? Is there moral value in each, and if so, is the weight of each equal to the others? Chapter 3 examines how different answers to those questions are philosophically motivated and how they make a difference to the structure of moral theories. This is a place where there are some important points of contact between metaethics and substantive moral theorizing. But here our main concern will be the forms of different theories. The question of form concerns a fundamental dimension of thinking about morality and moral theories.

The topic of chapter 4 is the relation between moral values and non-moral facts and properties, in particular, natural facts and properties. This is a way of asking the question, "Where (if anywhere) in the world is moral value?" We want to know whether moral value depends upon certain kinds of non-moral facts or properties, or whether it has a standing autonomous of them and what that could be. Imagine a particular action that is cruel because it was a deliberate wounding of another person just for the sake of harming that person, and the attacker took pleasure in this. Those are all parts of a factual description of the action in so far as they are the sorts of things identifiable and describable by observation and the sciences. What about the act being *wrong, because* it is cruel? Is the *wrongness* of it also a descriptive property – and how should we specify the relation expressed by *because?* If moral claims express attitudes or feelings do they still have certain kinds of regular relations with non-moral facts? If so, how is that to be explicated? We will also discuss the claim that morality has a theistic basis. Perhaps moral value has its basis neither in facts about the world nor in human feeling and attitudes, nor in rational principles; perhaps it has its ground in divine will or command. Chapter 4 takes up questions that can be stated fairly simply but which are very difficult to answer: what is the relation between moral value and whatever else there is; what is the relation between our non-moral knowledge and our moral commitments and judgments?

At the end of each chapter you will find questions for discussion and reflection. They are intended to sharpen your understanding of the issues in that chapter and help you connect them with other readings and the discussions in your course. There is also a list of the figures whose works and ideas were referred to, at the end of each chapter. In the lists, the first entry for each author is always a work that is explicitly referred to in that chapter. I have included in the lists a few works not actually quoted from but of sufficient importance to merit reference to them. There is also a glossary of terms used in the book. Each term that is in the glossary is in bold print the first time it occurs in the text. At the end of the book there is a complete bibliography of works quoted.

I hope that *Dimensions of Moral Theory* will be valuable to you in a very versatile way, along with whatever specific texts and topics you examine in your course. Some of the thinkers discussed are great figures you undoubtedly have heard of, while others are less famous but still quite important. Discussion of thinkers you are not studying in your course will still be topically relevant, and you are encouraged to read their works as well. This book is not meant to be a "field guide" to theories or a substitute for primary sources. Above all, it is intended to draw you into the distinctively philosophical dimensions of moral theorizing.

A note on terminology. You may be wondering if it matters whether you use the term "ethical" or "moral." The terms do have different etymologies and some philosophers believe it is important to distinguish between them and use them in different ways. Your instructor may have a view about this. I have tended to use the word "moral," as in "moral theory" or "moral value," mainly for consistency and stylistic reasons rather than special philosophical reasons. In the course of your study you may find that it is important to distinguish between the ethical and the moral. However, I have tried to develop the discussion in this book in way that does not depend upon a distinction between them.

Acknowledgments

The person I should like to thank first is Jeff Dean at Blackwell. He offered encouragement and guidance throughout the process of writing this book. I needed both, and I am very grateful to him, especially because this book is in some ways a departure from most books on moral philosophy or metaethics. Paul Markwick at St Andrews made detailed and very helpful comments on drafts of all of the chapters. Tim Chappell at Dundee and other readers for Blackwell did their job carefully and constructively and I extend many thanks to all of them.

I originally conceived the project while I was a Fellow at the Centre for Philosophy and Public Affairs at St Andrews. I participated in a weekly book seminar on moral philosophy with members of the Department of Moral Philosophy. That was a most enjoyable and instructive experience and it motivated me to try to write about moral theory in a way that highlights fundamental philosophical issues underlying it.

The Earhart Foundation very generously awarded me a Fellowship Research Grant, which supported several months of work on this project, including a visit to Australia, to present papers and pursue research there. Special thanks are owed to Adrian Walsh of the University of New England and Julian Lamont of the University of Queensland. Audiences at the University of New South Wales, Macquarie University, and the University of Melbourne are also to be thanked for their challenging questions and insights. Most of all, I would like to acknowledge my family, for more things than I know how to mention.

1 Objectivity and Subjectivity

Moral theories address concerns about practice, about what we should do. They often make specific claims about whether it is ever permissible to lie, about what rights people have, and about which duties take precedence over others when there are conflicts. They make claims about what is morally required and what is prohibited. However, when we reflect on the theories themselves we encounter many issues that do not directly concern what we should do or how we should judge acts or agents. For example, we may find that a theory presupposes that moral value is **objective**. It may hold that moral value is completely independent of the desires and interests people happen to have. In addition, moral theories often make claims or include assumptions about the nature of moral judgment. A theory may presuppose that in making moral claims we are expressing attitudes or feelings rather than reporting moral facts. Or it may hold that the correctness of moral judgments is always relative to the norms and standards of one or another culture or community. There are always commitments and assumptions in the background, if not stated explicitly, and they can be crucial to the form and content of a moral theory.

Issues concerning the nature and status of moral value and moral judgment are among the distinctively philosophical dimensions of moral theory. Even when they are not addressed explicitly the theorist's views about the metaphysics and epistemology of morality can often be discerned. Exploring those metaethical matters can give us a deeper and more textured understanding of a theory and can also give us crucial resources to work with in evaluating it. In this chapter we will look at some of the main positions and arguments concerning one of the most basic issues of all, namely whether moral value is objective or **subjective**.

Interpretations of Objectivity

What do we mean by objectivity? We speak of a person being objective (in his or her beliefs and methods), and we also talk about a truth or a fact being objective. Often when we say that people are being objective we mean that they are not biased or prejudiced, or that they are considering the relevant evidence carefully and impartially. They are not letting feelings or interests influence their views, and they aspire to attain a perspective that is the perspective of the impartial rational inquirer. In many contexts, being objective in this way is an important virtue. Think, for example, of the scientific explanation of a disease. We want to be sure that our understanding is accurate, detailed, responsive to the facts, and not corrupted by political or personal biases, for example. Or think of a detective trying to determine who committed the murder. It is of the first importance that he should proceed on the basis of evidence and supportable hypotheses, and not just arrest someone in order to satisfy the public or the District Attorney. Even if the detective acts on hunches they will be the hunches of a detective, of a person with the relevant skills and experience to know what to consider. In seeking to be objective our claims should be based upon our best efforts to arrive at the truth rather than upon what we would like to believe. If *we* are objective in our methods, then we will (so the reasoning goes) be better able to discover the objective facts. There is objectivity in respect to how we proceed and there is objectivity in respect to what we find out. The former can help lead us to the latter.

When we say that there are objective facts, or that a matter is an objective matter, what do we mean? One thing we might mean is that there is a way things are that is independent of how we conceive of them or describe them, that what there is in the world and what it is like do not depend upon what we think or say. Many theorists argue that moral values are not expressions of our concerns, interests, or feelings, and that because values are objective, there are objective moral reasons, objective action-guiding considerations. Some of them hold that rightness, wrongness, goodness, badness, obligatoriness, and other moral properties are independent of us. Value is not dependent upon feeling, decision, or perspective. On this view there are moral values that we can be (or fail to be) responsive to – we do not stipulate, choose, or invent them.

A good place to start an examination of objectivist conceptions of moral value is Plato's work. It is important both historically and philosophically. Our interest here is not in Plato's conception of justice or the ideal state, or any other specific moral issue. Our present concern is with the way in which Plato understood value to be real and objective and an object of knowledge. In fact, he thought that knowledge of good is the most important knowledge we can have.

Plato's was a conception of moral value as an impersonal, absolute reality existing apart from any objects of sense perception and apart from human desires and feelings. It is the measure that we refer to when we claim that an act or a person is good. It is not a measure of our own making. He wrote:

> And beauty itself and good itself and all the things that we thereby set down as many, reversing ourselves, we set down according to a single form of each, believing that there is but one, and call it "the being" of each.[1] ... And we say that the many things beautiful things and the rest are visible but not intelligible, while the forms are intelligible but not visible.[2]

The form of the good has a standing in its own right. Moral value is not grounded in or determined by feeling, social custom, human convention, or any other source besides its own independent, intrinsic nature separate from objects in the natural world.

When we seek to understand the ways in which various things in the world are good, we are working our way towards an understanding of the good, something that each good thing approximates to some extent. But the good itself has a nature separate from the things in the world that are good things. None of the latter is a complete, perfect realization of good, and their goodness is judged in relation to the absolute standard. When we are thinking about good, about value, we really are thinking about an object of the understanding. Our knowledge of good can always be enlarged, made more complete and more coherent. Value, in this sort of view, is not dependent upon *valuing* as a human activity. It is not our valuations that determine what is good and what is not. We need to have knowledge of good to make correct valuative judgments. We can be correct or incorrect in those judgments because good is an impersonal, objective reality.

Our understanding of good is often distorted by bias, ignorance, or misrepresentation. If we think of value in terms of our likes and dislikes and our desires, we will be distracted from a true comprehension of value. With discipline, education, and reflection we can come to a true and accurate understanding of what good is in its own right. (This process of education is what much of the *Republic* is about.) That knowledge is of supreme importance for acting well and living well. The best thing a human being can do is act in light of knowledge of the good.

Thinking about value is an undertaking that is as fully objective as any other attempt to understand the nature of reality. In experience and inquiry we find that many different things have similar properties. For example, cattle, birds, fish, and rodents are all animals. In Plato's view, they are all animals by virtue of some real property that they share: animality. That property is no less a reality and an object of the intellect than the creatures we encounter in nature. In perception we encounter this, that, and the other particular animal, but the intellect can grasp and comprehend animality in its own right. Genuine knowledge is not a matter of arriving at reliable generalizations about animals; it is a question of having a penetrating understanding of what it is to be an animal. We do not perceptually encounter animality, but it is what is understood when we have knowledge of what it is to be an animal.

Consider another example. Having knowledge of geometry is much more than being able to recognize triangles, squares, and other figures. It is being able to demonstrate what are the properties of various figures on the basis of a grasp of first principles. Those principles and the propositions that are proved from them are objectively true, even though we never encounter a perfect geometrical figure in sense experience. Still, we know what are the properties of isosceles triangles – we know what it is to be such a thing, what makes each isosceles triangle one of those rather than something else. Perfect geometrical figures are not objects of perception, but they are objects of the intellect.

The same is true of good. If a man is a good man, and an action is a good action, and a social arrangement is good, there is some property they all share, by virtue of which each is good. When we truly say of something that it is good, we say it because it is – because that property is exemplified by it. It is goodness that makes it true of each of those things that it is good. It is goodness itself that we need to comprehend in order to have a complete and accurate understanding of what it is for things that are good to be good. It is the ideal, distinct from its instances. That is what thinking about value, when it is disciplined and informed, seeks to understand. Judgments of value are no more matters of opinion or social convention than judgments about geometrical figures. They are **cognitive** matters about which our judgments are either true or false.

The Platonic conception is not a relic of ancient philosophy, something interesting only as an exhibit in a history of ideas museum. In the twentieth century G. E. Moore developed a view quite similar to Plato's in some ways. He wrote:

> But whoever will attentively consider with himself what is actually before his mind when he asks the question "Is pleasure (or whatever it may be) after all good?" can easily satisfy himself that he is not merely wondering whether pleasure is pleasant. And if he will try this experiment with each suggested definition in succession, he may become expert enough to recognize that in every case he has before his mind a unique object, with regard to the connection of which with any other object, a distinct question may be asked. Every one does in fact understand the question "Is this good?" When he thinks of it, his state of mind is different from what it would be, were he asked "Is this pleasant, or desired, or approved?" . . . he has before his mind the unique object – the unique property of things – which I mean by "good."[3]

Moore was a Platonist in the sense that he held that intrinsic value is real, objective, and an object of cognition distinct from everything else. Like Plato, Moore held that we do not decide what is good, nor do we base judgments of goodness on feeling or taste, or personal interest. We can make objective, true judgments concerning moral value, and when we correctly think of something as good, we have before our minds a property or an entity that we can discriminate from all other properties or entities. True judgments of what is good are made true by virtue of the fact that those things *are* good.

However, Moore denied that good can exist as a separate, wholly independent reality. It is one thing to say that good is real and is something in its own right and another thing to say that it can be found all by itself. (Texture is distinct from weight and from material composition, but it cannot exist all by itself as texture alone, not being the texture of something.) Moore held that good is real, but not a standalone reality. This means that the presence of good depends upon the presence of other things, but it is not *identical* with any of them. Perhaps we can conceive of a world in which there are only intrinsically good things – but that would still not be a world in which there was goodness alone. It would be a world in which there would be only things that are good things. When we are aware of good, we have direct awareness, (which Moore called "**intuition**") of the presence of a real property distinct from all other properties, but not definable in terms of anything else. We will have much more to say about this issue in chapter 4 when we discuss the relation between moral value and natural properties. Right here our concern is to point out that Moore's view involves important Platonist elements and assigns moral value a fully objective status. To understand moral judgment, Moore held, we must see that true moral judgments answer to objective moral value. Judgments of value are responsive to a reality that makes them true (or false). They answer to something and do not have their basis in subjectivity. It is the reality of value that is authoritative for claims about what is good.

Despite significant differences between Plato's and Moore's moral theories and the way they conceive the role of moral value in a human life, they share a commitment to moral value as a fully objective constituent of reality. They also share the view that there are things in the natural world that are good but goodness itself is not a natural phenomenon. It has its own nature and cannot be analyzed into any other components, elements, or terms. It is not something we perceive with the senses or encounter as an item in the physical world. This may make it sound like "good" is the name of a peculiar object we might hunt for and discover somewhere. But objectivity should not be construed narrowly, only in terms of being something concrete that one might point to in one's visual field and say, "you see it; it is over there" or something like that. Good is apprehended cognitively, not by the senses. In addition, a key element of views of this kind is that when we know what *good* is we know what *it* is. Good is not a complex of other things such that it can be analytically decomposed. When we truly say of something that it is good we are attributing a certain distinct property to it.

There are interpretations of the objectivity of moral value quite different from Plato's and Moore's. Indeed, a version of moral objectivity without moral value as an object or an entity was developed and defended by Kant. He held that moral claims are objective, but this is because they satisfy certain formal rational conditions, not because they refer to a mind-independent reality. Kant held that moral requirements are determined by our own reason. Moral value does not have its source in our interests, feelings, or desires. Neither is it a feature or property of the world, such that knowledge of the world would include knowledge of it. The authority of objectivity is the authority of our own rationality. He held that moral value has its ground in practical reason and, "since moral laws should hold for every rational being as such, the principles must be derived from the universal concept of a rational being generally."[4] The objectivity of the fundamental principle of morality, what Kant called the "**categorical imperative**," is the objectivity of "universally valid necessity."[5]

This is an account of objectivity in terms of what is rationally required, where this is determined by the formal structure of rational principles. In using the categorical imperative as a criterion for the moral permissibility of a principle of action, we are employing a standard that is fully objective in the respect that meeting that standard shows that the principle could be endorsed by any rational agent. A categorical imperative can be impartially universalized because it is not conditioned by whatever desires, passions, or interests the agent has. Those differ across different agents. However, there are principles whose rationality is not conditioned in those ways. They have authority for us simply as rational agents.

Moreover, only rational beings are capable of morality because only rational beings have "the capacity to act according to the conception of laws, i.e., according to principles."[6] It is the universality and necessity of rational principles that make for moral objectivity. The objectivity of morality is not a matter of there being a normative reality "out there." Our own rationality is the source of objective moral demands upon us. As agents, as beings who are capable of acting on different kinds of motives, we are aware in our own experience of the difference between answering to obligation and answering to inclination. These are not just different motives, but different sources of motivation. When we answer to the former, we are responding to the unconditional authority of practical reason. The objectivity of moral claims is based upon different sorts of considerations than the objectivity of empirical claims, but it is full-fledged objectivity. It is the objectivity of rational necessity.

The Kantian view should not be perceived as watered down objectivity compared to Plato or Moore's conceptions. Kantian objectivity does depend on us, but only in the sense that we are rational agents and it is our ability to universalize principles of action that determines the morality of an action. While moral principles are grounded "in" us they are not subjective, any more than mathematical truths are. Moral judgments are objectively true or objectively false. Kant too, is a cognitivist about moral judgments. These are not claims we make on the basis of feelings of approval or as expressions of a certain attitude. There is an objective criterion for the correctness of moral claims, and that criterion is formulated by reason. It is not external to us or imposed upon us. Indeed, Kant argued extensively that any appeal to a value or interest or concern external to practical reason itself would subvert morality. It would make it impossible for there to be categorical imperatives – imperatives that are necessary just by virtue of their rational structure, rather than on account of an end to be achieved or an interest to be pursued. Thus, Plato and Moore differ from Kant in holding that moral value is part of the constitution of reality, and when we have knowledge of it, we have knowledge of something independent of us. All three, however, agree that moral value does not have its basis in human subjectivity or the ways we happen to think and feel. Our task, as moral agents, is to order our thinking in accord with objective considerations of value.

Some of the basic elements of the Kantian view have recently been developed in an approach called "**constructivism.**" John Rawls, who sees his own work as substantially influenced by Kant, writes:

> The search for reasonable grounds for reaching agreement rooted in our conception of ourselves and in our relation to society replaces the search for moral truth interpreted as fixed by a prior and independent order of objects and relations, whether natural or divine, an order apart and distinct from how we conceive of ourselves.[7]

The moral facts are constructed, arrived at, by principles of moral reasoning. Rawls's own view is not simply an exposition of Kant's view; it is an original development that acknowledges its debt to Kant. Still, it helps us see how the Kantian approach differs from those theories in which moral objectivity is a matter of what things exist.

Another contemporary philosopher, Thomas Nagel, has developed and defended a view of objectivity that is centrally concerned with attaining an objective standpoint. In this view, the emphasis is on objectivity as an aim of a method of reflection that enables us to see what is true concerning value. As we more fully approximate to objectivity, we achieve a clearer and more accurate conception of moral reasons. He defends the view that:

> propositions about what gives us reasons for action can be true or false independently of how things appear to us, and that we can hope to discover the truth by transcending the appearances and subjecting them to critical assessment. What we aim to discover by this method is not a new aspect of the external world, called value, but rather just the truth about what we and others should do and want.[8]

From the objective standpoint we are able to see what are the best reasons for action. Attaining objectivity with respect to reasons for action should also influence our motives. There are action-guiding normative truths. "The view that values are real is not the view that they are real occult entities or properties, but that they are real values: that our claims about value and what people have reason to do may be true or false independently of our beliefs and inclinations."[9] When we understand value, we have an understanding of what is good or right to *do*. What is brought into view by the objective standpoint are not just reasons for me. They are reasons that can be expressed in normative propositions that are objectively true or false.

Plato and Moore held that moral value is a feature of reality independent of what we believe and feel, and that moral judgments are true, or false. Thus, they are moral **realists**. There are true moral judgments, and they are true by virtue of moral value being among the things that exist and are objects of knowledge. Nagel claims to be a realist as well. He calls his version "normative realism." It is the view that normative reality is a matter of what kinds of reasons there are independent of what we think and feel, not what kinds of objects there are. Commenting on Nagel's view, Christine Korsgaard writes, "Some contemporary realists, such as Thomas Nagel, have argued that realism need not commit us to the existence of curious metaphysical objects like Plato's Forms or Moore's non-natural intrinsic values."[10] "We need only believe that reasons themselves exist, or that there are truths about what we have reason to do."[11] In order for there to be objective reasons there need not also be something *else* in virtue of which there are objective reasons. We can say that moral values are real without that implying that they are items on a list of what there is in the world.

Kant's view is an objectivist view, but it is arguable that it is not (clearly, anyway) a realist view. According to Kant, moral considerations are objective by virtue of passing a formal test of universalizability. There are objective considerations of what reason requires, but he is not committed to moral value as an *object* of reason. Objective moral principles are formulated or constructed by practical reason from its own resources. He did not hold that moral value exists as a reality in its own right apart from the exercise of reason.

The issue of whether moral realism must be committed to moral values as constituents of reality is a good example of how the interpretation of the most fundamental categories of moral thought is itself a disputed matter. The contrasts we have just identified illustrate this. Each theorist we have mentioned maintains an objective conception of value, but their accounts of the metaphysics of moral value differ in important ways. Nevertheless, despite the differences between Kant, Plato, Moore, and, more recently, Rawls, Nagel, and Korsgaard, they all agree in rejecting the view that moral values are part of the natural order studied by the empirical sciences. We cannot "get at" moral value by somehow reading it off of empirical facts or defining good in terms of the objects and properties we encounter in the natural world.

John Stuart Mill argued that moral value can indeed be understood in empirical terms. We can achieve a correct conception of value on the basis of naturalistic considerations, principally facts about what people desire for its own sake. He held that if we correctly understand human action, we see that ultimately the overall aim of all we do is pleasure. Pleasure alone is desired for its own sake and *only* for its own sake. In Mill's theory, facts about the psychology of subjects are objective facts that support and explain objective considerations of value. After all, if X is what people desire for its own sake and only for its own sake, it would seem that that is a powerful reason for thinking that X is valuable and should be promoted, that X is good. Isn't it objectively better to experience pleasure than to experience pain – because pleasure is objectively better than pain? The resulting view is that pleasure is what has objective value, and thus there is a reason to strive to maximize it. The key point of present concern is not the claim that pleasure has intrinsic value, but that value is objective. Mill did indeed have a **hedonist** theory of value. He thought that pleasure was the good. Right now, what is important about Mill is the way in which he sought to give an account of moral value on the basis of empirical facts. This is a version of **naturalism**, a topic we will discuss from some additional angles in chapter 4.

Value, in Mill's view, is real but it is not distinct from the natural world in the way that Plato, Kant, and Moore argued that it *must* be. A basic issue regarding objectivity is what kinds of considerations there are for moral judgments to respond to, to take into account; what kinds of considerations could make moral judgments true or false? In some theories they are facts about value as a certain kind of entity or property, or facts about value as rationally constructed, or empirical facts about human beings and the natural order. When we say that values are objective we are saying that value judgments are true or false by virtue of stating or failing to state what is in fact the case as regards moral value. Where the theorists we have been discussing differ is over how to interpret and explicate "what is in fact the case" as regards moral value. They all agree in being objectivists.

Mill thought that part of his project as a theorist was to demystify morality and put it on a firm and empirical basis. He thought that the way to do this was to show that value can be explained in terms of what is desired for its own sake and only for its own sake. If there is something such that all other things are ultimately desired for the sake of it, then there is a reason to pursue it as good. He claimed that this was true of pleasure. The normative claim has an objective basis grounded in facts about what people desire. In addition, it is a matter of fact whether action (or practice) A produces (or tends to produce) more overall good than action (or practice) B, or whether they produce the same amount. Thus, judgments about what has value and about what to do are factual judgments.

There is another important account of the objectivity of moral value that differs from all the ones we have considered so far. Its most influential version is due to Aristotle. According to Aristotle, the way to understand morality is in terms of what is excellent human activity and what is the best life for a human being. He held that there is an objective conception of the proper function of essential human capacities. Among them is the capacity for practical rationality, rationality that is action-guiding. Well ordered practical reason grasps and appreciates what is good and that appreciation motivates the agent to act accordingly. The good in this view is not an object or entity we encounter, and neither is it a construction out of rational principles or a specific psychological state, such as pleasure. Given the distinctive constitution of human nature, there are certain kinds of activity that make for human excellence, and the agent with practical wisdom has sound, reliable judgment about what acts are required. There are objective conditions of a flourishing life, of living well and doing well, given what human beings *are*. There are goods proper to human beings on account of their distinctive nature. What constitutes acting well and doing well is not a matter of what an agent happens to desire. There are *correct* desires, and these are desires for what is genuinely good for a human being.

The agent with the virtues has sound, action-guiding understanding and enjoys acting in accordance with it. The virtuous agent is someone in whom reason and desire are in agreement in such a way "that what reason asserts is what desire pursues."[12] "The unconditionally good deliberator is the one whose aim expresses rational calculation in pursuit of the best good for a human being that is achievable in action."[13] This person has a type of intelligence that is "a state grasping the truth, involving reason, concerned with action about what is good or bad for a human being."[14] The way in which moral good is realized in a person's life is through acting in ways that express correct understanding of what is choiceworthy. There are certain core virtues that are crucial to an excellent life. (We will say much more about the virtues in chapter 3.)

In all rational action agents aim at what they take to be good, and it is rational for any human being to have a coherent, guiding conception of how to live. We can pursue false goods, and even think that we are living well when we are not if our judgment is corrupted. The virtuous agent, however, has a true conception of human good and leads an excellent life through acting in ways that realize that conception. The central conception of Aristotle's view is the notion of an excellent life for a human being. He does not identify a distinctive category of moral value or moral obligation, and that is one way in which his view differs from, say, the views developed by Kant and Mill. To be sure, he is concerned with what is required by practical rationality in order to act well and to live well. But for Aristotle there is not a clean break between the moral and the non-moral. We will comment further on this issue below in this chapter and in other chapters. Our present concern is with how his understanding of the objectivity of value differs from other conceptions of objectivity.

We could say that, like Mill, Aristotle has a conception of moral value that is grounded in nature, but it is a quite different view of nature and of value. Aristotle held that there is a mode of activity proper to a human being, and that is very different from Mill's claim that it is a completely general fact about human beings that they desire pleasure for its own sake, and thus there is a reason to maximize pleasure. These differences make a great deal of difference to the character of moral judgment and reasoning, as we will see later on.

The debate about how to interpret the objectivity of moral value remains very much alive. The conceptions we have looked at have been particularly influential, but they are not the only ones. They do, though, supply valuable resources for thinking about the issue and they give us a sense of how broad is the range of interpretive possibilities.

It is important to see that the issue is not only whether moral value is objective, but also how to characterize what makes for its objectivity. You should consider just what an advocate of moral objectivity is claiming. Does moral objectivity imply that: (a) moral claims have truth-values (that is, they are true or false); (b) the morality or immorality of X-ing is independent of people's beliefs about whether it is moral or immoral; (c) the morality or immorality of X-ing is independent of anyone's desires or feelings; (d) the morality or immorality of an act or situation depends entirely upon its natural properties; (e) its morality or immorality is distinct from its natural properties; or (f) something else, or some combination of (a) through (e)? It is in the details of the answers to those questions that you will find the merits and defects of this or that specific position on the issue.

Monism and Pluralism

In theories such as Kant's and Mill's there is an explicit attempt to identify *the* fundamental moral principle or criterion of right action. In Kant's theorizing the good will alone is unconditionally good and what makes it good is that it wills in accordance with the moral law *because* it is the moral law. The categorical imperative (the moral law) is the fundamental principle of right action. It is the sole criterion of right action. In Mill's theory, good is interpreted in terms of pleasure, and accordingly, the principle of utility is the criterion of right action, and it is the sole criterion. There are many pleasures, but the good that is pursued in morally right action is a single good. Each of those theories is an example of **monism** concerning moral value − the view that there is just one type of moral value. And each theory maintains that there is a single fundamental moral principle.

It is not necessary that a moral theory settle upon just one fundamental value or one fundamental principle even if the theory maintains that moral value is objective. Moore, for example, held that while good is the object of moral thought, there are several intrinsic goods, and some are greater goods than others. He wrote: "By far the most valuable things, which we know or can imagine, are certain states of consciousness, which may be roughly described as the pleasures of human intercourse and the enjoyment of beautiful objects."[15] Each of these is an objective and irreducible good, and he held that there are other goods as well.

Aristotle's moral philosophy could be interpreted as a type of **pluralism**. While he held that there is an overall good for human beings, he also maintained that there are diverse virtues, each of which enables us to realize different excellences. The value that is realized in acting courageously is not just the same value as that realized in acting justly, or honestly, or magnanimously. We can give a general account of virtue and of the overall excellence of a human being but: (a) there are distinct virtues that are responsive to distinct value considerations; and (b) there is no single, absolute principle or criterion of right action. There are distinct moral values and there is no specific, fixed way to order them because there is no single, common measure of them. The goods realized by virtuous activity are not homogeneous. The person with practical wisdom is able to judge and deliberate on the basis of a correct overall understanding of human good, but that does not require a single, fundamental principle of moral judgment.

It is illuminating to look carefully at book 10 of Aristotle's *Nicomachean Ethics* and its culminating discussion of happiness and the best life. Does he unequivocally settle on either the contemplative life or the practical life as the best life for a human being? Is this an example of pluralism with respect to what constitutes human perfection, the overall good for a human being? While it is part of Aristotle's view that there is an overall good for human beings grounded in the distinctive capacities constitutive of human nature, he seems to acknowledge that it may not be possible to fully pursue excellence in a practical life *and* also pursue the excellence of a contemplative life. In any case, even if we interpret Aristotle as a pluralist, he is a pluralist in the sense that he believes that there are distinct, irreducible *goods*; value is to be understood in terms of good as the basic category.

There are also pluralistic approaches that hold that there are multiple fundamental sources of value. For example, writing on the issue of whether moral value is of just one type, Nagel says:

What we need most is a method of breaking up or analyzing practical problems to say what evaluative principles apply, and how. This is not a method of decision, but more usually it would simply indicate the points at which different kinds of ethical considerations needed to be introduced to supply the basis for a responsible and intelligent decision.[16]

And: "I believe that value has fundamentally different kinds of sources, and that they are reflected in the classification of values into types. Not all values represent the pursuit of some single good in a variety of settings."[17] For example, among the kinds of value we might recognize are utility (or welfare), autonomy, **perfectionist** considerations (perfecting or fully actualizing one's nature), and rights considerations. There could be others as well, and it is a helpful exercise to try to think of what they might be. The duty to do what one can to keep a promise may involve a value that is distinct from the value of aiding those in distress. These might concern distinct kinds of value, not just distinct *goods*.

If moral value is pluralistic then there will be important and difficult questions about how various value considerations are related. If there are irreducibly distinct values, how do they jointly figure in moral judgment and reasoning? This is not exactly the same issue as the familiar issue of conflicts of duty. For example, a Kantian who takes the categorical imperative to be the one and only principle of morality might encounter conflicts between, say, aiding those in distress and keeping a promise. An agent has made a promise, which, let us suppose, can only be fulfilled by proceeding without delay. However, the agent encounters a situation in which another person needs aid, but helping will make it impossible to fulfill the promise. A strategy for dealing with conflicts is needed, but the alleged conflicts arise (the Kantian would argue) because sometimes multiple obligations make claims on us, not because there are irreducibly different moral values. The issue of how to resolve conflicts of obligation is genuine and difficult, but the issue of different values making claims on us is another (related) matter with its own complexities. For example, is the duty to be beneficent based upon the same sorts of grounds as the duty to be honest, or just?

If values are pluralistic it may be possible to order them, indicating which values take priority over others. This is not to say that they can be measured in some straightforward quantitative way – if they could be measured against each other, there would be a common criterion for all judgments of moral value, but that is just what pluralism denies. Pluralism is the view that there are different ends or virtues worth pursuing for their own sakes, or distinct intrinsic goods, or distinct and irreducible principles (or all of these). These cannot be straightforwardly compared, even if there are grounds for the judgment of their value. (Different pleasures *may* be comparable, but pleasure and other goods are not comparable.) Still, the pluralism of value would not imply that there is no coherent way to weigh different types of moral considerations. For example, considerations of fairness might take precedence over considerations of utility, or certain rights might take priority over others. This, of course, would need to be shown in a carefully reasoned manner, since pluralism is decidedly not the same thing as making moral judgment arbitrary.

Pluralism implies that there is no single measure or standard of value that will decide all conflicts of obligation or determine the weights of all the values at issue in a situation or a judgment. While that may appear to be a difficulty for pluralism, the approach may be motivated by the recognition that there *are* different kinds of value considerations, each with a claim to objectivity. Careful reflection might reveal that attempts to reduce all value to one dimension or source are forced, and misrepresent the reality of value. Perhaps pluralism is a *response* to the difficulty, not the origin of it. We will not pursue the monism–pluralism issue in depth right here, though it is appropriate to mention it because of its significance and its important connections with the debate about objectivity.

As an interim summary, let us note some of the key points that have been made so far.

1   There are several different accounts of objective moral value.
2   On one interpretation, moral value is objective in the sense that it exists independently of everything else in the world, and it is knowable by reason or the intellect. Things in the world can more or less approximate it, but it is a reality in its own right. (Plato)
3   On another interpretation, moral value is objective in the sense that it is an object or property and even though its presence depends upon the presence of other things. It is not itself a natural object or property. It is real and irreducible. (Moore)
4   On another interpretation, moral value is objective in the sense that its character is determined by universal and necessary ra-

tional principles. (Kant) In a variant of the view, moral principles and moral facts are constructed by a process of rational reflection. (Rawls)

5   On another interpretation, moral value is construed realistically even though values are not items in or features of the world. Rather, normative realism is explained in terms of what are genuine moral reasons from the objective standpoint. (Nagel)

6   On another interpretation, moral value is objective in the sense that moral value is constituted or determined by natural facts (about human desires, interests, or other psychological states, or preferences as revealed in behavior). (Mill, and various versions of utilitarianism)

7   On another interpretation, moral value is objective in the sense that, given the constitution of human nature, there are intrinsic goods for human beings that can be understood by reason and realized by the virtuous exercise of rational capacities. (Aristotle)

8   All of the interpretations of moral objectivity are cognitivist accounts of moral value.

9   Moral value may be objective and pluralistic.

We end this section with a word of caution. All objectivists agree that moral value is objective in the sense that moral judgments are cognitive judgments, i.e. they are literally true or false. They disagree over what *makes* them true or false. They differ over the proper account of what constitutes the objectivity of value.

This Way to Subjectivism

To many people it seems plain that moral values are objective. When we say that cruelty is wrong we are (they claim) stating an objective truth about cruelty. It is wrong, and that is not a matter of opinion, feeling, or personal choice. Nor is it a matter of cultural custom or linguistic convention. The judgment that cruelty is wrong responds to and reports the fact that it is. It is just as objective as the fact that cats are mammals. It is not always easy to tell what is morally good or bad or right or wrong, but moral thought answers to something objective.

On the other hand, to many theorists it seems equally clear that there are no objective moral values, or even that *there could not be* objective moral values. What in the world (in a quite literal sense) could an objective value *be?* In a pithy, influential statement of this view, John Mackie has written:

> If there were objective values, then they would be entities or qualities or relations of a very strange sort, utterly different from anything else in the universe. Correspondingly, if we were aware of them, it would have to be by some special faculty of moral perception or intuition, utterly different from our ordinary ways of knowing everything else.[18]

Mackie is suggesting that there is something exotic about objective value, and that it would be unlike anything else we encounter and that we could not encounter it with the faculties by which we encounter everything else. Both metaphysically and epistemologically, values would be quite extraordinary. He refers to this as the "queerness" of values.[19]

There is another important criticism of objectivism and this one is based upon the notion that moral considerations are generally thought to be action-guiding. They have *practical* significance. For example, the fact that something is red or is four feet long or two hundred miles from the equator has no action-guiding significance in its own right. That an act is wrong is a weighty reason against *doing* it. That it is obligatory is a weighty reason for *doing* it. Or we could say that whatever it is that *makes* it wrong or obligatory is an action-guiding consideration. For example, if it is wrong because it is harmful, then that is a reason not to do it. If an action is obligatory because doing it fulfills a promise, then that is a reason to do it. Moral considerations make, or at least *should* make, a difference to action, to what we do, or ought to do, and not just to what we *believe*.

In Mackie's view, if there were objective values or moral facts, they would be objects of reason or perception or of some special faculty for detecting them. He thinks that is more than enough mystery. Yet objective values are even worse off than that. Supposing we could encounter or detect them, we would just be encountering or detecting the fact that something is the case (is wrong, obligatory, permitted, etc.). But just coming to know something or being aware of something is not itself action-guiding. How could the recognition or the belief that something is the case be action-guiding just on its own? It seems that without desire, or feeling, or concern – something other than just belief or knowledge – there is nothing to motivate action. To many critics, objectivism seems to leave the issue of moral motivation and the practical significance of moral considerations either unexplained or altogether inexplicable. This is one of the most important objections to moral objectivism.

A classic source for this type of critique of moral objectivity is David Hume. He wrote:

> The end of all moral speculation is to teach us our duty; and by proper representations of the deformity of vice and beauty of virtue, beget correspondent habits, and engage us to avoid the one and embrace the other. But is this ever to be expected from inferences and conclusions of the under-standing, which of themselves have no hold of the affections nor set in motion the active powers of men? They discover truths: but where the truths which they discover are indifferent, and beget no desire or aversion, they can have no influence on conduct and behaviour. What is honourable, what is fair, what is becoming, what is noble, what is generous, takes possession of the heart, and animates us to embrace and maintain it. What is intelligible, what is evident, what is probable, what is true, procures only the cool assent of the understanding; and gratifying a speculative curiosity, puts an end to our researches.[20]

The charge is that objective values and knowledge of them would be inert. As objects of the understanding, they have no motivational energy. Therefore (the reasoning goes), moral considerations must have a ground in human feeling, desire, or interest. They must have a ground in something that can drive and direct action. An object or property or beliefs about objects or properties cannot do that.

A corollary of this is the view that when we make moral judgments we are expressing a stance or an attitude or a feeling, and not reporting facts. We are approving or disapproving, or exhibiting an interest or an aversion. But we are not saying what is the case. That is not to say that beliefs have no role. Beliefs about what in fact is the case are indeed important to moral thought, even when it is interpreted as subjectivist. After all, it is in respect to facts, acts, and situations that we *have* moral views and stances. It is because Jones's attack on Smith was unprovoked and violent that we condemn it and judge it to be wrong. But there are no distinctively moral facts or objective values. Moreover, they are not needed. We can give adequate explanations of moral judgment and experience without them. Moral judgments can be explained by reference to sensibility, desire, and interest. There are good factual explanations about why morality matters to us. However, those explanations need make no reference to moral facts or objective moral values.

Let's look at a bit more of Mackie's critique. He says that we can ask:

> about anything that is supposed to have some objective moral quality, how this is linked with its natural features. what is the connection between the natural fact that an action is a piece of deliberate cruelty – say, causing pain just for fun – and the moral fact that it is wrong? It cannot be an entailment, a logical or semantic necessity. Yet it is not merely that the two features occur together. The wrongness must somehow be "consequential" or "supervenient"; it is wrong because it is a piece of deliberate cruelty. But just what *in the world* is signified by this "because"?[21]

He then says:

> How much simpler and more comprehensible the situation would be if we could replace the moral quality with some sort of subjective response which could be causally related to the detection of the natural features on which the supposed quality is said to be consequential.[22]

We might think that the sort of objectivism developed by Mill has the best chance of the objectivist options, since it does not postulate values as entities with a metaphysically distinct status. Moreover, his view does not make the sorts of assumptions Aristotle made about the proper ends of human action and about human excellence, or the claims Kant made about rationally necessary principles. We might say that once the non-moral facts are set, so are the moral facts. The latter can be completely accounted for in terms of the former. It can seem like a quite straightforward, almost scientific approach. There are facts about what people desire, and about what pleases people, and those are the basis for moral judgments. But Mackie is pointing out that this attractive appearance is *mere* appearance. After all, just what is the relation between those facts and moral values? How is it to be specified?

It is implausible to argue that "good" can be simply *defined* as "pleasant," "conducive to pleasure," or "desired." Does "good" mean exactly the same as any of those? If the relation between natural properties and good is not definitional (not "semantic" as Mackie put it), then just *how* is goodness related to, or consequent upon, natural properties? Perhaps the most plausible explanation is that value just is not objective and instead it depends upon attitudes, feelings, or concerns that we express or project onto things. We might say that we approve of what is pleasant and therefore regard it as good and seek to promote it. But it is the approval that is the basis of the valuation and it is the approval that moves us to act. The goodness of pleasure is not a matter of objective value.

The upshot of the critique so far is as follows. (a) The objectivist is committed to (allegedly) strange entities and faculties. (b) The objectivist has the task of explaining how those entities are related to natural properties and entities. (c) The objectivist leaves it a mystery how moral facts or objective values could be action-guiding, since in themselves they involve no intrinsic relation to desire, passion, or interest. (d) Moral beliefs and practices can be adequately explained without any commitment to the existence of objective values. We can explain the ways in which acts and practices are morally good or bad, or why characteristics are virtues or vices, without cluttering up the picture of what there is with objective values. We have, for example, a quite clear idea of what cruelty is, and we are quite confident in our judgment that cruelty is morally wrong.

Suppose that our judgment that cruelty is wrong is based on sensibility, on our finding it repugnant. Why isn't that enough to support the judgment that it is *wrong*? Why is that not a plausible, adequate explanation? It also helps us understand how a moral judgment is related to action. If you find something repugnant and you are repelled by it then you are supplied with at least some reason not to do it and reason to criticize or condemn it. Your feeling that it is repugnant will move you to condemn it or try to stop it, and will impede you from being motivated to act cruelly. Objectivism is obscure on the practical dimension of moral considerations and subjectivism is *clear* in respect to it. It does not just win by default. It avoids the intractable difficulties of objectivism, and it gets the explanatory job done. So argues the subjectivist.

Mackie's argument for subjectivism is particularly interesting because he acknowledged that most people regard moral value as objective. He argued that "ordinary moral judgements include a claim to objectivity, an assumption that there are objective values in just the sense in which I am concerned to deny this."[23] His view was that people typically *think* that moral judgments report moral facts, but they are mistaken in thinking so. Given this, Mackie's own theory is actually a cognitivist approach – an approach that maintains that moral judgments are literally true or false – but Mackie argues that they are all false because there are no objective values. Thus:

> the denial of objective values will have to be put forward . . . as an **"error theory,"** a theory that although most people in making moral judgements implicitly claim, among other things, to be pointing to something objectively prescriptive, these claims are all false.[24]

It is an error to think that values are objective, but there are several reasons why people persist in the error and do not recognize it as such. (You might try to hypothesize about what those explanations are. Mackie presents them in chapter 1 of *Ethics: Inventing Right and Wrong.*) One reason is that it seems to many people that in order for moral considerations to have the kind of weight and authority they have, they must be objective.

Most subjectivists are **non-cognitivists**. They do not believe that moral judgments are either true or false, but that they *express* attitudes or feelings. Mackie argued that because most people (without committing themselves to one or another philosophical theory) assume that moral judgments are cognitive judgments, we should acknowledge that, while also (philosophically) arguing that those judgments are false. They are not meaningless; they are not incoherent. But they are not true. To the extent that moral judgments presuppose objective values, they are false.

Philosophers sometimes take the view that philosophical reflection vindicates common-sense views. It supplies justification for things we already believe. That is how Kant saw his project of moral theorizing. He claimed that it was part of the "common rational knowledge of morals" (a phrase he uses repeatedly in *Foundations of the Mataphysics of Morals*) that certain duties are unconditional. He also held that the ordinary person, with no help from theory, was typically capable of ascertaining moral duties. Kant saw his philosophical theory as an account of a morality that was familiar to the plain person through his consciousness of moral duty. Mackie had a quite different view of what philosophical reflection reveals about our common-sense moral beliefs. It reveals that they are false, because at the level of critical reflection we find that what we typically presuppose about the status of moral value cannot be true. Both, however, claim to get their theorizing under way from a starting point that is furnished by the common-sense view, and they both (in different ways) take the common-sense view to have objectivist commitments. That is not automatically a presumption in favor of objectivity, but it is an important consideration that merits careful examination.

Subjectivity and Sentiment

The denial that moral values are objective is not the same as a denial that they are important. A critic of objectivism may take morality to be just as weighty a matter as the objectivist. The moral subjectivist may be keen to show that we will and should continue to strongly condemn cruelty, malice, dishonesty, and so forth. We will and should carry on admiring and encouraging honesty, benevolence, and fairness. Nor is this just a matter of psychological inevitability. The subjectivist is not saying "Look, we cannot help making moral judgments, so there is no problem if there are no objective values." Rather, the claim is that a subjectivist account of moral value fully accounts for moral judgment, evaluation, and reasoning. It may be that the very same things will matter to us morally even though our account of the status of moral values will not be objectivist.

When we say that judgment is subjective or based upon feeling we do not necessarily mean that it is just a matter of taste. (We might mean that, but we probably do not.) How seriously can we take someone who says: "We don't approve of cruelty, and almost no one does. It is pretty awful and we want as little of it as possible. But that's just how we *feel*. That doesn't show that cruelty is wrong. It just shows we don't like it." That seems an inaccurate rendering of the situation. Preferring kindness to cruelty is not comparable to, say, preferring mussels to clams. The subjectivist can argue that for a claim to have a subjective basis is not the same thing as for it to have a weak basis or a basis in personal taste. Unless one's sensibility is exceptionally hardened or perverted, it just cannot recognize cruelty as morally acceptable. After all, doesn't it seem just as plain, just as certain to you, that cruelty is wrong as that iron is a metal?

Whether you elect to get up off the couch and rake the leaves, or decide to just stay there dozing, is a matter of how you feel. Whether you should help the person who was just knocked down by a car in front of your house is not a matter of how you feel in the same way. Morality is still full-force, full-fledged morality and need lose nothing by being based upon human subjectivity. The point is not that the desire to get up off the couch is unsupported by reasons, but the choice to help the injured person *is* supported by reasons. After all, you may decide to rake the leaves after having thought about and concluded that it is a good idea; there are good reasons to do it. Still, in the case of helping the injured person, it seems that there is a type of claim upon you that is just absent in the first case. Moral reasons have a certain authority, even if interpreted in subjectivist terms. It is a mistake to assume that moral subjectivism is a strategy designed to call into question the genuineness of moral value. It may be intended as a strategy to *explain* it, rather than explain it away.

It is of course open to the subjectivist. to also use anti-objectivist arguments as a way of calling into question the genuineness of moral value. There are versions of subjectivism that claim to maintain the genuineness of morality and there are versions that call it into question. The subjectivist and objectivist *may* agree that unless moral values are objective, they are less than genuine and have less authority for us than objective moral values would have. This kind of subjectivist maintains that only objective values could have the authority moral considerations need, and there are no objective values. Therefore, moral considerations lack the authority many people think they have. The objectivist may claim that subjectivism necessarily subverts moral value. According to the objectivist, subjectivist attempts to explain and preserve the genuineness of morality in a non-deflationary way are failures and cannot succeed in explaining why helping the injured person has a stronger claim on us than raking the leaves. But the attempt to preserve the weight and authority of morality is something the subjectivist may want to undertake.

Hume, for example, presented some of the most influential arguments against objective values, but not with a view to undermining morality. While he explained moral values as grounded in human sentiment, he made it plain that that does not mean being subjective in a person-relative way. He writes:

> The notion of morals implies some sentiment common to all mankind, which recommends the same object to general approbation, and makes every man, or most men, agree in the same opinion or decision concerning it.[25]
>
> And though this affection of humanity may not generally be esteemed so strong as vanity or ambition, yet, being common to all men, it can alone be the foundation of morals, or of any general system of blame or praise.[26]

According to Hume morals are grounded in a common human sensibility and human beings constitute a single moral community. Within that community there can be argument, criticism, and changes of view motivated by reflection and by finding out facts about people and situations. Thus, subjectivism can allow a role for reason while still denying that values are objects detected by reason or are constructions of reason (as in Kant's view). The person who does not see the wrongness of cruelty is making a moral mistake. This is not someone of whom we are willing to say, "Oh well, everyone has their own taste and their own values. If he thinks cruelty is morally all right, there is no error in that, even if we happen to feel differently." Hume's point (and the point of contemporary philosophers influenced by Hume) is that taking cruelty to be wrong is not just or merely a matter of how we happen to feel – even though the judgment that it is wrong has its basis in sentiment.

We judge what to do, what practices to accept, and which to discourage on the basis of what elicits our admiration, our gratitude, our esteem, our contempt, our fear, our distrust, and so forth. Moral judgments ultimately have a basis in the passions and in desires, in something *felt*. Also, they render the judgments practical by giving them motivating energy. It is feeling that moves us, even when it is feeling informed by factual knowledge and structured by reasoning.

Adam Smith, another great eighteenth-century moral philosopher, wrote:

> If virtue, therefore, in every particular instance, necessarily pleases for its own sake, and if vice as certainly displeases the mind, it cannot be reason, but immediate sense and feeling, which, in this manner, reconciles us to the one, and alienates us from the other.[27]
>
> But though reason is undoubtedly the source of the general rules of morality, and of all the moral judgments which we form by means of them; it is altogether absurd and unintelligible to suppose that the first perceptions of right and wrong can be derived from reason, even in those particular cases upon the experience of which the general rules are formed.[28]

Smith's account of moral judgments differs in a number of ways from Hume's but he agrees that sentiment is the basis of value. These sentiments can be proper or improper, felt in due measure, or not, and so forth. This is by no means "anything goes" subjectivism. There are certain ways we should think and decide that are made known to us by our responses and our feelings. Following feeling is not simply a matter of doing what one likes or acting in whatever way one feels like acting. Rather, sentiments are crucial to our having the right sort of receptivity to moral considerations, and we can reflect upon them and assess whether they are appropriate or not.

In ordinary practice, we certainly do make moral judgments that we are expected to support. We argue and we reconsider and revise our views. We think that some things are definitely, unquestionably wrong and others right, and so forth. And we give reasons for our views. These are all features of moral life and experience. For thinkers like Hume and Smith, the problem was not "how can morality be saved or reconstructed if values are subjective?" The question was more like this: "how are we to understand moral value and the various dimensions of moral experience, judgment, and argument?" Their answer was in terms of human sentiments. In that respect, it was in terms of subjectivist considerations.

Subjectivism and Skepticism

In philosophy a position is a **skeptical** position if it calls into doubt the claims made concerning a certain issue. For example, if you have reasons to doubt that perceptual knowledge-claims can be adequately justified, you are a skeptic with respect to perceptual knowledge. If you have reasons for doubting that causality is a real, objective relation between things in the world, and you believe that causal judgments reflect habits of mind rather than objective causal facts, you are a skeptic with respect to causality. If you have reasons for doubting that there are objective values, then you are, at least in some respect, a moral skeptic. That is why subjectivism can be said to be a skeptical view.

We need to be cautious, though. In denying that there are objective values, the subjectivist is adopting a skeptical stance in one sense, even if, like Hume and Smith, he claims that subjectivism explains all that genuine moral values can be and need to be. This might sound confusing. But remember, it is possible to be a skeptic about objective values without being a complete skeptic about morality. The subjectivist need not be saying that there isn't *really* morality or that moral values are illusory or unimportant. The subjectivist may be saying that the authenticity of morality does not rest on, and does not need, objective values.

We should distinguish between claiming that there are no moral values and claiming that there are no objective moral values. There certainly seem to be moral values, even if they are not objective. It is conceivable that all claims that there are objective moral values are false, though this leaves plenty of room for values and for different interpretations of them. (Mackie, who claimed that all moral judgments are false because there are no objective values, also held that we make moral judgments and that doing so is of the first importance. They need to be interpreted in subjectivist terms. But that does not diminish them.) This is not just to say that as a matter of sociological fact there is always one or another prevailing morality. It is the claim that the genuineness of moral judgment does not depend upon the existence of objective values. So, a subjectivist (we can imagine Hume in this role, for example) can argue that these moral claims rather than those are correct, but not by answering to objective values.

Of course, it is open to the subjectivist to go further, and to argue that moral notions are all somehow pathological, illusory, or otherwise lacking in authority – none of them are correct or valid except in the sense that people happen to think they are or cannot give up thinking in those terms. That would be skepticism that doubted that moral considerations have any claim on us. But that is a rare and (in ways you might think about) quite implausible view. When considering moral skepticism it is important to be clear about just what it is that is being denied. It might be the validity of the prevailing values of one's society or culture; it might be that there are objective values; it might be that there are any moral values at all.

For many theorists there is an important connection between objectivity and truth. If there are objective values then at least some beliefs, claims, and statements about value are literally true. They are not just true "around here" (in this community, culture, or time). They are not true because we say that they are – we say that they are because they are. If values are subjective, then value claims are not literally true or false in the way the objectivist understands truth and falsity. This is a complex issue for the following reason. Suppose we are subjectivists about moral value. We are confident that there are no objective values and that moral judgments do not report moral facts. They are either not true or false at all, or they can only be said to be true or false *given human desires, feelings, and responses.* Still, we may go on saying things such as "it is true that cruelty is wrong" and "it is true that generosity is a virtue" and "it is not true that it is morally all right to make a deceitful promise." We will have a stance toward moral judgments by which we take them as seriously as if they were literally true or false, even though we do not believe that they are moral-fact-stating – there are no moral facts for them to be true or false *in virtue of.* For the subjectivist, what makes for moral truth is something about us, about the form and context of human sentiment and concern.

You might find this a little bit suspicious, as though the subjectivist is trying to have it both ways. If there are no objective values or moral facts, then how can moral statements actually be more than expressions or projections of feeling or attitude? Let's make a distinction here. The subjectivist can argue that there is no harm in saying that there are moral truths if what we mean is that we accept certain moral statements as true, and would argue for them, and would argue against statements that contradict them. What more is needed for moral truth? Why should a realm of objective values also be needed? Think of Hume's universal sentiments, and the commonality of human interests and concerns. Don't they supply an adequate basis for morality? Can't we plainly see that some practices are morally abhorrent, others are morally admirable, some characteristics are virtues and others are vices? Subjectivism about value does not obliterate those distinctions; it puts them on a certain kind of basis. Or so it has been argued.

An important type of subjectivism holds that if we look at the way we use moral language we see that it exhibits many of the characteristic marks of cognitivism. It has the *form* of language that is used to make statements that are literally true or false. We say that it is true that we should not punish the innocent, just as confidently and meaningfully as we say that it is true that there are high winds on Mount Washington. But upon reflection and analysis, we find that there are no objective moral values or objective moral facts (such as the fact that *punishing the innocent is wrong*). That does not expose moral discourse as a fraud. It shows that a subject matter that is subjective in nature can exhibit the same reason-giving, objection-answering, evidence-requiring features of genuinely cognitivist discourse.

It may be helpful to notice some of the ways in which the general form of this debate is analogous to the debate concerning free will and determinism. There is a position in that debate called *compatibilism*, according to which free will and moral responsibility are consistent with determinism. The view holds that even if all of our actions were causally determined there is still a place for talk of free will and still a place for moral responsibility because what matters is not simply whether or not our actions are causally determined, but what *kinds* of causes they have. If you are making your way to the end of the diving board in preparation for a showy dive in order to impress someone watching from poolside, and you land on someone in the water because you had your eye on your admirer rather than on where you were diving, then you are responsible for injuring the swimmer. You were acting on the basis of your intentions and your beliefs, and not being forced to do anything; you were inexcusably inattentive. Now, suppose you are carefully making your way to the end of the diving board, and survey-ing the pool in order to make sure it is safe to dive, but someone sneaks up behind you, pushes you off, and you land on someone in the water and injure that person. Your falling into the water is the cause of the injury but you are not at fault. The blame lies with the person who shoved you. You did not jump voluntarily, and you were not negli-gent.

The compatibilist says that both sequences of events are the prod-ucts of causes preceding them but they are importantly different kinds of sequences, and the difference makes a difference to the assignment of responsibility and blame (and the appropriateness of punishment, if that is an issue in the case). According to the compatibilist, what mat-ters with respect to responsibility is not whether an action is caused or uncaused, but whether the cause centrally includes the agent's wants and beliefs. Was the behavior an enactment of the agent's conception of what to do, or the effect of coercion or compulsion? That is what is crucial to voluntariness and responsibility. This is a way of arguing that we can make all of the relevant distinctions concerning responsi-bility, blame, voluntariness, coercion, ability, and the like without *first* (or ever) showing that there is a type of freedom of will that is both real *and* inconsistent with determinism. The language of praise and blame, accountability and voluntariness, and the associated notions apply even if all our actions are causally determined.

Analogously, the subjectivist can argue that we can make all the relevant distinctions between correct and incorrect, or sound and un-sound moral views. We can sort out well supported from poorly sup-ported views, and we can see how one moral view is an improvement over another, and the like, without first (or ever) showing that there are objective values or moral facts. The subjectivist insists that there is no cost to moral practice or to the authority of moral considerations if we interpret value subjectively.

The objectivist is unimpressed by the subjectivist's lack of concern on this issue. The objectivist will suspect that the subjectivist's confidence about the genuineness of moral considerations cannot be vindicated or sustained. The subjectivist has to either find a stronger ground for moral claims or admit that the apparent genuineness of moral considerations is *merely* apparent. If moral values are an expression or projection of affect, feeling, or attitude – if they are reflective of a stance rather than the grasp of something objective – then what makes for morally correct or right feelings or attitudes? If it is "attitude all the way down" doesn't that seriously threaten the genuineness of moral judgments?

If the subjectivist wants to say, "It is attitude all the way down, but that doesn't stop us from persisting in moral evaluation," that is one thing. We noted earlier that this is really no more than saying that there are practices we engage in and are not about to give up. On the other hand, the objectivist is unconvinced that those practices can be *what we take them to be*, if the subjectivist interpretation of them is correct. The notion of moral truth, the notion of a view being more correct than another, the notion of moral understanding (and that it might improve or worsen) all seem to presuppose and require that moral beliefs *answer* to something, and do not merely *express* something. Otherwise, evaluating moral claims is on no firmer ground than evaluations of games, in order to ascertain which is better.

Within the rules of a game we can say that this is allowed and that is not. We can say that one move was well played and another was not. But we cannot say that cricket is a better game than baseball, or darts is a better game than croquet, since ultimately those judgments are a matter of attitude all the way down. We can make many factual judgments about which games are more complex or more demanding of mental or physical skill, and the like. Think, for example, of the difference between card games for young children and poker or bridge. That still does not resolve the issue of which is the *better* game in some objective sense. It depends on what you want from the game. According to the objectivist, the subjectivist is mistaking the standing of evaluations we can make *within* the practice of using a set of norms for the standing of those norms themselves. He is saying that the practices will only *look* like moral reasoning and argument and will not be authentic unless there are objective values.

Similarly, critics of compatibilism insist that it is an unstable and untenable position. Defenders of free will argue that determinism is determinism. If an individual's act was causally necessitated, then it was unavoidable, and not a free act. Even if the agent was doing what he wanted, chose, or intended – the want, the choice, the intention were all fully determined. Acting on the basis of an intention *feels* different from being coerced or acting compulsively, but again, determinism is determinism. If there is to be genuine free will and moral responsibility they are not compatible with determinism. The hard determinist critic of free will agrees, and maintains both that determinism *is* true and that, because it is true, free will and moral responsibility are illusory. Like the defender of free will, the defender of determinist incompatibilism insists that the types of causes do not make a difference. To the moral objectivist, the type of subjectivism we have been describing seems like a kind of compatibilism about moral truth. The view holds that there are no moral facts or objective values, but we should treat moral discourse as though its claims are true or false. The objectivist might get frustrated and demand to know which way the subjectivist wants it. Are moral claims true or false, or are they expressions of attitude?

There are views that explicitly deny that moral claims are cognitively significant. A. J. Ayer wrote:

> If a sentence makes no statement at all, there is obviously no sense in asking whether what it says is true or false. And we have seen that sentences which simply express moral judgements do not say anything. They are pure expressions of feeling and as such do not come under the category of truth and falsehood.[29]

Note that Ayer does not say that moral judgments express propositions *about* the speaker's feelings. In that case, they would have cognitive content and they would be true or false. They would be factual reports about psychological states. Consider the difference between "I (or we) strongly disapprove of that" and "That's wrong." Ayer says that claims of the latter sort are expressions of feeling and do not have propositional content that could be true or false. Some versions of subjectivism, such as Ayer's, are "officially" non-cognitivist. His is an **expressivist** view, according to which in making moral claims we are expressing feelings or attitudes and not reporting facts or making statements that are to be evaluated as true or false.

What about accounts such as Hume's or Smith's? They plainly are not objectivist interpretations of moral value, but neither are they "thinly" expressivist in the way that Ayer's is. Hume, for example, says that in making a moral judgment a man must: "depart from his private and particular situation, and must choose a point of view, common to him with others; he must move some universal principle of the human frame, and touch a string to which all mankind have an accord and symphony."[30] Smith writes extensively about what he calls the "impartial spectator" and he says that it is "only by consulting this judge within, that we can ever see what relates to ourselves in its proper shape and dimensions; or that we can ever make any proper comparison between our own interests and those of other people."[31] By adopting the point of view of the impartial spectator we can ascertain what are the proper sentiments and their proper degrees. We can see ourselves as others see us and we can see whether our sentiments are fitting.

It is fair enough to call both of these views subjectivist and expressivist in so far as the raw material of moral judgment is sentiment. Still, Hume and Smith seem to be saying that there are roles for impartiality and for reason in determining what are the proper sentiments. This is not "blind" expressivism by any means. Again, the upshot seems to be that on views such as Hume's and Smith's, if the agent does not think that cruelty is wrong, he is *mistaken*.

One possibility is to argue that on such views the person who does not think that cruelty is wrong makes a *moral* mistake, but not a factual mistake. Simon Blackburn writes:

> To "see" the truth that wanton cruelty is wrong demands moralizing, stepping back into the boat, or putting back the lens of sensibility. But once that is done, there is nothing relativistic left to say. The existence of the verdict, of course, depends on the existence of those capable of making it; the existence of the truth depends on nothing (externally), and on those features that make it wrong (internally).[32]

Blackburn seems to be saying that within morality we can make judgments that we regard as true or false, but their truth or falsity is internal to morality and not a matter of reporting or representing objective facts external to the moral point of view. Is this a way of showing that moral judgment is sufficiently cognitivist in character to count as being true or false? Or is this a way of saying that moral judgment is not officially cognitivist, but there is no loss to morality by its not being so? This is a sophisticated type of expressivism – but can any expressivism, no matter how sophisticated, ultimately be more than "thinly" expressivist?

Relativism

We have been discussing the view that moral values have their basis in human sentiment or desire. There is another important rival to objectivism that holds that values are relative to the norms of different times and places. This is **relativism**. It is open to the relativist to argue that relative to a set of norms and beliefs we can say that judgments are true or false, but relativism denies that there is an objective or neutral standpoint from which values can be ascertained or constructed. There are no objectively true or false moral claims. There are different norms and conventions, and there is no special reason to think that any of them has a universal basis. Most forms of relativism maintain that differences in culture or context explain much of the diversity. The relativist can admit that there could be a universally shared morality, but that would be a historical, contingent matter. It would just happen to be the case that everyone agreed on moral matters, even though there is nothing objective to agree on. The claim that there is no objective, universal, enduring objective basis for morality is fundamental to relativism.

Given the characterization of relativism we can say that Hume and Smith were subjectivists without being relativists. Hume spoke of "the *party* of humankind."[33] Morality, he thought, is grounded in common human sentiments and is not group-relative or person-relative. It is everyone's morality. Smith wrote, "We should view ourselves, not in the light in which our selfish passions are apt to place us, but in the light in which any other citizen of the world would view us."[34] Their versions of subjectivism involve impartiality and universality in a way that is not typical of relativism. The latter maintains that what is permissible, what is admirable, what is prohibited, and so forth, is internal to a culture or a community, and that there is no impartial standpoint from which the norms can be assessed. Within a social or cultural world there is a public moral discourse and there are shared values that the community enforces and sustains. For those in the community, acceptance of those values is not merely discretionary. Those values shape and inform their world in such a way that the values may seem to them to be objective. But they are not. There are many variants of relativism, but for all of their variety, the core is that the correctness of moral judgments is relative to the subjects who make them. Different cultures have different moral values and engage in different practices, and even the history of any given culture may show that there have been quite striking changes in moral belief and practice. The human world is a world of historical, social, and cultural contingency. Amidst that contingency arise moralities, connected with various traditions, ideals, and guiding concerns.

It is not the mere fact that there are cultural differences that makes a case for relativism. After all, the fact that groups may have different beliefs about some matter is not in itself evidence that there is no objective fact of the matter. If a society believed that there are no prime numbers that would not motivate genuine doubts about whether there are prime numbers. It would prompt interesting questions about the mathematical concepts and understanding of that society. Similarly, if a culture insists that all illness is due to demonic possession, that does not, in its own right, raise a challenge to the best supported scientific explanations of illness. What else besides the fact of difference points *away* from objectivity? The critic of objectivism might argue that the fact of so much persistent, irresolvable diversity of moral views gives us some reason to doubt that there are objective values. With regard to values in particular, there seems not to be a basis for claims of objectivity. (Contrast this to the context of explaining illness.) Moreover, it can be argued that we can supply quite good accounts of different cultures' moral views in terms of various different features of those cultures (their histories, circumstances, needs, etc.) without any reference to objective values.

Important features of morality shared by many cultures could be explained in terms congenial to relativism. For example, moral rules against certain practices, such as murder, are explainable in terms of needs and interests that almost any culture or community has, though there is no objective rightness to the prohibition of those practices. Also, every society has some system for allocating benefits and burdens among its members, purportedly with a view to the good of the society, despite the remarkable variety of practices, institutions, and rationales for them. Every society has practices concerning treatment of, regard for, and grieving for those who have died, but there is not some "right" way to do this. The relativist can acknowledge moral commonality but is likely to argue that: (a) to the extent that there are moral commonalities, they can be explained without postulating objective values; (b) differences between moralities can be adequately explained in terms of cultural, historical, and other differences; (c) there is no method for ascertaining what are the alleged objective values. Any claims to objectivity would be "inside" one or another culture and the value claims would be shaped and informed by that culture.

It would be much too quick to conclude that there are no objective values from only the premise that different cultures have different moralities. What is crucial to the argument is what *explains* the fact that there are these different moralities. Mackie, for example, argued that: "The actual variations in moral codes are more readily explained by the hypothesis that they reflect ways of life than by the hypothesis that they express perceptions, most of them seriously inadequate and badly distorted, of objective values."[35] Indeed, Mackie goes to some length to identify different reasons why people do tend to think their moral claims are objective – though they are in error about this.[36] The truth is that correctness of judgments is always *relative to* different customs, practices, languages, valuations, and ideals.

The relativist does not require that at the level of actual moral practice and belief we cease to regard moral claims as being true or false. However, at the reflective level, we can see that truth and falsity are relative and could not be otherwise. This need not be threatening to morality unless one thinks that the only possibilities are that either morality is objective or there just is no such thing as morality. But why, the relativist asks, should we think that? Why should the genuineness and significance of moral values depend upon their being universal and objective?

Relativism may seem appealing as a particularly effective way to make a case for tolerance. In denying that there is some objective measure for morality, relativism appears to be non-judgmental. However, there is nothing intrinsic to relativism that says that diversity is a good thing, or that not judging the values of others is a good thing. Those claims, were they to be made, would be made "inside" one or another value system. They would not have objective standing. Relativism is consistent with the most lethal dogmatism and closed-mindedness, as well as being consistent with valuing diversity and encouraging tolerance. It is a thesis about the status of values, not a thesis about which values people should have. In fact, it would be problematic for a relativist to argue that the thesis objectively supports tolerance. To do so would be inconsistent. The relativist can be tolerant, welcoming towards difference, non-judgmental and non-interfering – but for reasons other than the commitment to relativism.

In responding to relativist arguments, objectivists can point out a number of things. First, the fact of difference, even persistent difference, does not show that there are no moral facts of the matter. Perhaps a great deal of time, learning, and experience is needed in order for people to bring objective values into view. "Objective" does not mean obvious or self-evident, and there is no special reason to think that moral matters are any more transparent than many others. The disagreements may in principle be rationally resolvable even if in fact we do not succeed in resolving them.

Second, even if there are good explanations for why there are diverse moral systems, they do not show that there are no objective values. The existence of those explanations is consistent with there being objective values, and even with people thinking that there are none. There may be sociological and historical explanations for why certain societies have the moral systems they have. That does not exclude the possibility that there are objective values or moral facts. Perhaps our moral theorizing is in an underdeveloped state, and with time and effort, we will see more clearly that there are objective moral judgments.

Third, it may be an important part of our understanding of moral considerations that they are *not* "local," *not* relative in the sense that if we believe that indentured servitude, or slavery, or causing pain just for sport are wrong, then presumably we believe they are bad practices because of what *they* are, not just because of who *we* are. If we believe we have reasons for morally objecting to these things then we might wonder why those reasons do not extend to wherever these things are found. If we say, "Well, it's wrong for us, but not wrong for them, given their values," in just what sense do we mean it is *wrong for us*? Can we be altogether accommodating with respect to values, thinking that because a certain moral practice is at home in another culture, that validates it? This is not a proof of the objectivity of morality but it does point to an objectivist aspiration of a great deal of moral thought. Justifications may not be cogent to others because of their beliefs and values, but if they are genuine justifications, then if others are informed and rational, they should be able to understand them and see the merit in them. If they fail to see the merit in them, it may be their fault, rather than an indication that the claims lack objectivity.

In any case, how, as relativists, are we to specify what are the relevant groups to which values are relative? If the answer is that the whole of humanity is the relevant group, then we are back to Hume and Smith's subjectivism, which is not relativist in the same way as many explicitly relativist theories. What if it is a smaller group? Which

group? Isn't each of us a member of many different groups, communi-
ties, affiliations, and so forth, and can't these be specified in many
different ways? This difficulty for relativism may not be fatal, but it is
serious and it needs to be addressed in a careful manner. In addition,
suppose a subgroup refuses to accept certain moral conceptions and
remains steadfast in its own moral commitments. Is that evidence that
its commitments are as supportable as the prevailing ones? Or, contra-
riwise, is the minority mistaken because it is diverging from the prevailing system? (Were Southern abolitionists in the early 1800s wrong?
Are critics of mutilation punishments for theft morally mistaken because tradition sanctions those practices in some societies?) How small
can a minority be? Why not regard moral values as relative to individual persons? Can we even make sense of the notion that action A is
wrong for person P only if person P accepts norms on which action A
is wrong – and that there is no non-person-relative reason for P to
accept those norms?

The claim that values are person-relative is quite different from the
claim that morality involves subjective commitment. Even if values are
objective, acting morally involves commitment on the part of the individual agent, and neither facts nor reasons can "make" an agent do
the right thing. The dutiful Kantian agent is not muscled around by
objective reasons but is resolute, by a disposition of will, to act rightly.
That sort of resolve (or virtuous dispositions, or seriousness about promoting utility, etc.) is personal, but not in a way that indicates the
relativity of moral values or moral reasons.

The objectivist can also point out that objectivity allows for a measure of variability. The position does not require a commitment to
fixed, exceptionless principles or requirements. Objectivity primarily
concerns the status of values and moral claims, rather than whether
they ever have exceptions. There may be objective moral reasons in
favor of the general requirement to be honest but this is compatible
with there being objective moral considerations that permit deception
in certain kinds of cases. The objectivist can respond to differences in
conditions and context but remain an objectivist by remaining true to
values that have objective standing. A good general example of this
can be drawn from **utilitarian** theory. The theory holds that the best
overall state of affairs is what we should seek to promote, but there will
be different ways of doing this, according to circumstances. In one
setting, the market and extensive private property rights may be the
best system, while, in another setting, a quite different economic and

social arrangement may be best. That is not to say that utilitarianism is actually a type of relativism, but that the application of the principle of utility can be objectively responsive to differences in conditions and circumstances.

Finally, the issue we identified concerning the specification of groups to which values are relative is an important burden on the relativist. What are the relevant specifications for the relativist account of morality, and what is the rationale for those specifications? In the absence of those, the relativist may have some arguments against moral objectivity, but will not be well positioned to make a case for relativism as the alternative. Reasons to doubt one view are not automatically reasons in favor of a specific alternative view. The latter must have merits of its own, and must be able to respond to objections.

Where Now?

We have looked at a number of views of the status of moral value, ranging from Platonism to skepticism and relativism. These positions are not simply fixed options to choose from. It would be better to see them as attempts to answer fundamental questions about the status of moral value and the nature of moral judgment – questions that remain very much alive and in dispute. One way in which the debate about the status of moral value is important is that it has a direct bearing on whether there is moral knowledge and what kind of understanding (if any) is involved in having moral views. It is relevant to whether moral views can be literally correct or mistaken, and whether moral claims assert facts or express feelings or attitudes, or whether they are relativistic and domesticated to social and cultural settings.

With this background concerning the status of moral value, we turn to some equally important questions concerning moral *agents*. In addition to an account of moral value, a theory needs a conception of the nature of moral agency, and an account of moral motivation, in order to be complete. In developing those, we need to address crucial questions about the relation between self-interest and morality, the relation between pleasure and moral value, and the extent to which agents have (or lack) control over the moral worth of their actions. These are questions of moral psychology, and we turn to them in chapter 2.

Questions for Discussion and Reflection

1   Explicate the differences between Kant's account of the way in which moral value is objective and Mill's conception of its objectivity. What sorts of philosophical motivations led them to arrive at such different views?

2   In what ways, if any, do different interpretations of moral value as subjective undermine or threaten moral judgment and the weight or authority of moral considerations? Why might a moral objectivist insist that subjectivism is a threat to genuine morality?

3   What are the key differences between Hume's appeal to human nature in explaining moral value and Mill's appeal to human nature in explaining moral value?

4   In what ways, if any, should the objectivity of moral considerations (if, indeed, they are objective) help secure agreement on moral matters? How important is the issue of moral agreement and disagreement to the debate about objectivity? Is it important to moral agreement that there should be such a thing as moral *knowledge*?

5   Relativists appeal to a number of different considerations in making the case for moral relativism. What are the strongest considerations in favor of it? What are the strongest objections to relativism? How can they be met by the defender of relativism?

6   Aristotle is critical of Plato's conception of the good at the same time that there are some important affinities between their conceptions of moral value and human nature. Explain the main points of comparison and contrast between their views regarding these matters.

Thinkers and Their Works, and Further Reading

Aristotle: *Nicomachean Ethics*
A. J. Ayer: *Language, Truth and Logic*
Simon Blackburn: "How to Be an Ethical Antirealist"; "Moral Realism"
R. M. Hare: *The Language of Morals*; *Freedom and Reason*
David Hume: *An Enquiry Concerning the Principles of Morals*; *A Treatise of Human Nature*

Immanuel Kant: *Foundations of the Metaphysics of Morals*; *Critique of Practical Reason*
Christine Korsgaard: *The Sources of Normativity*
John Mackie: *Ethics: Inventing Right and Wrong*
J. S. Mill: *Utilitarianism*
G. E. Moore: *Principia Ethica*
Thomas Nagel: "The Fragmentation of Value"; *The View from Nowhere*
Plato: *Republic*
John Rawls: "Kantian Constructivism in Moral Theory"; *A Theory of Justice*
Adam Smith: *The Theory of Moral Sentiments*

Notes

1   Plato, *Republic*, trans. G. M. A. Grube (Indianapolis: Hackett Publishing Company, 1992), VI, 507, 180.
2   Ibid.
3   G. E. Moore, *Principia Ethica* (Cambridge: Cambridge University Press, 1994), p. 68.
4   Immanuel Kant, *Foundations of the Metaphysics of Morals* (Indianapolis: Bobbs-Merrill, 1976), p. 28.
5   Ibid., p. 34.
6   Ibid., p. 29.
7   John Rawls, "Kantian Constructivism in Moral Theory," in *Moral Discourse and Practice*, ed. Stephen Darwall, Allan Gibbard, and Peter Railton (New York: Oxford University Press, 1997), p. 248.
8   Thomas Nagel, *The View from Nowhere* (New York: Oxford University Press, 1986), p. 139.
9   Ibid., p. 144.
10 Christine Korsgaard, *The Sources of Normativity* (New York: Cambridge University Press, 1997), p. 40.
11 Ibid., p. 40.
12 Aristotle, *Nicomachean Ethics*, trans. Terence Irwin (Indianapolis: Hackett, 1985), 1139a, 25.
13 Ibid., 1141b, 13—14.
14 Ibid., 1140b, 4—5.
15 Moore, *Principia Ethica*, p. 237.
16 Thomas Nagel, "The Fragmentation of Value," in *Mortal Questions* (New York: Cambridge University Press, 1985), p. 139.
17 Ibid., p. 132.

18 John Mackie, *Ethics: Inventing Right and Wrong* (Harmondsworth: Penguin, 1977), p. 38.
19 Ibid., p. 38.
20 David Hume, *An Enquiry Concerning the Principles of Morals*, 3rd edn, ed. L. A. Selby-Bigge (Oxford: Clarendon Press, 1975), p. 172.
21 Mackie, *Ethics: Inventing Right and Wrong*, p. 41.
22 Ibid.
23 Ibid., p. 35.
24 Ibid. Bold type added.
25 Hume, *An Enquiry Concerning the Principles of Morals*, p. 272.
26 Ibid., p. 273.
27 Adam Smith, *The Theory of Moral Sentiments*, ed. D. D. Raphael and A. L. Macfie (Indianapolis: Liberty Fund, 1984), p. 320.
28 Ibid.
29 A. J. Ayer, *Language, Truth and Logic* (New York: Dover, 1952), p. 108.
30 Hume, *An Enquiry Concerning the Principles of Morals,*. p. 272.
31 Smith, *The Theory of Moral Sentiments*, p. 134.
32 Simon Blackburn, "How to Be an Ethical Anti-realist," in *Essays in Quasi-realism* (New York: Oxford University Press, 1993), p. 178.
33 Hume, *An Enquiry Concerning the Principles of Morals*, p. 275.
34 Smith, *The Theory of Moral Sentiments*, pp. 140—1.
35 Mackie, *Ethics: Inventing Right and Wrong*, p. 37.
36 See Mackie's discussion of what he calls "patterns of objectification" in *Ethics: Inventing Right and Wrong*, chapter 1.

2 Moral Theory and Moral Psychology

There is no single, brief definition of moral psychology. Among its concerns are questions about the nature of moral motivation and the role of reason in motivating agents to act morally. Does motivation to act rightly depend upon sensibility, desire, or other aspects of our nature? The relation of happiness to virtue, the relation of self-interest to morality, and the moral significance of pleasure are other key issues of moral psychology. These are fundamental aspects of moral agency and experience, and every major moral theory includes or presupposes moral psychological claims. We need a realistic and plausible conception of moral agents and we need it to fit with our conception of moral value. Otherwise, the overall coherence of our view will be undermined, or at least less strong than it could and should be. We begin our discussion with the issue of how and why agents might (or should) be moved by moral considerations.

Moral Motivation

Morality concerns practice, action, what we *ought to do*, and not only judgment and evaluation. If a theory cannot account for how moral considerations are action-guiding it is lacking in a respect that is just as important as its account of the locus and nature of moral value. This was evident in the subjectivist critique of objectivism. We shall begin our discussion with an illustration that raises some of the main questions about moral motivation.

Suppose you are driving on a road that is not frequently traveled and you see a motorist who has pulled over and obviously has a flat tire, and this person has a cast on one arm. It is not likely that others will be driving by any time soon, and it is plain that he cannot change the tire by himself. What might (or should) motivate you to help this person? After all, there are many different possible motives for assisting. What are some of them?

1   You feel compassion for this person, so you help him because you do not want him to remain in distress.
2   You were in a similar situation once yourself, and a friendly stranger helped you, and you feel that in some way, you owe it to this person to do the same. It is a kind of gratitude that moves you, even though this is not the person who helped you.
3   You wonder if maybe there will be some reward for helping. It is an expensive looking car and a well dressed motorist, and you think your chances of getting some money for helping are not bad.
4   You see that this person needs help, and you are motivated by that consideration in its own right. You believe you ought to help, because this person needs help, and you are in a position to be of assistance. You are motivated by the thought that it is the right thing to do. What you take to be the reason for helping is also your motive for helping.
5   You imagine yourself in the other person's position; you see that you would want someone to help you; and you are motivated by seeing the situation in that light. (This is not just the same thing as compassion or feeling sympathy for the person in need.)
6   You do not feel like stopping; you do not want to get dirty; you could not care less whether this person lives or dies by the side of the road, but you worry that feelings of guilt might gnaw at you if you do not stop and help.
7   You see this as an opportunity to miss an event you really do not wish to attend, and you can explain your absence by saying how you stopped and helped a stranded motorist. The situation is a good excuse to do what you most want to do (miss the event) while looking like you are a caring person.
8   You recognize the person, and though you would not otherwise stop to help, this is someone you like, so you stop.
9   You recognize the person, and you are pretty sure he will recognize

you, and you will look bad if you do not stop to help. So, concern for your reputation motivates you to help.

10   The motorist is a well known person, and you think of the opportunity for attention and credit as the helpful stranger who rescued him.

The list could be made much longer, but it gives an idea of the diversity of possible motives. They are not only different motives; they have different sources. Some have their ground in sentiment or feeling, some in desire, some in reason, and some in considerations of self-interest. Also, some are distinctively moral motives and others are not. (Stopping just to avoid feeling guilty if you did not stop is not a case of being motivated by a moral consideration. You just do not want to feel badly later on.) Our present interest is in the question of what is a morally sound or proper motive and what is its source. We might say that in every case the *reason* to stop and help is that person needs assistance. However, it may be that reason alone is not sufficient as a motive to move you all the way to action. You may understand the reason to help, but be unmoved to do so.

One important view is that your recognition of moral reasons to stop, independent of how you feel or what you are worried about, can indeed have sufficient motivational efficacy. This is the view that there need be no motivation external to moral reasons themselves. You do not *also* need to want to act that way or see that it is to your benefit to act that way, for example. Kant held a view of this type. In fact, Kant held the view that if you stop and help for other than moral reasons, your action (though it is a good thing to do) lacks *moral* worth. It is better to help than not to help, but the moral worth of the action depends upon whether you do the right thing because it is the right thing. In acting morally we are not *properly* motivated by the incentive to bring about a desirable·or favorable state of affairs, and we are not *properly* motivated by sentiment, passions, or self-interest. Kant argued that if the requirements of morality were, so to speak, "held hostage" to the presence of motivations having a source outside of reason, then whether we fulfilled those requirements would depend upon our feelings or interests and not upon the fact that they are moral requirements. That would undermine the authority and genuineness of moral obligations.

According to Kant there is a fundamental connection between rationality and moral motivation. Actions conditioned by the presence of desires, passions, or interests lack moral worth, because in so acting we fail to respond to what is rationally required just because it is rationally required. Reason can ascertain what is morally required, and reason alone can be a sufficient motivation to do what is required. Moreover, we all *do* (he thought) recognize the distinctive character of moral obligations. Each of us is aware of a distinction between obligation and inclination as sources of motivation. Just by virtue of being agents with practical reason, we can recognize that some actions are rationally necessary in their own right while others are necessary for the sake of some end or interest we happen to have. Actions that are necessary in the latter way are only hypothetically imperative. Morality concerns actions that are categorically imperative – that is, required by reason alone, independent of motives or ends supplied by feeling or desire.

The question of whether reason on its own can supply sufficient motivation is one of the most disputed questions of moral psychology. Kant developed one of the most influential formulations of the notion that *reason can be practical*, that it can motivate action on its own. It should be unsurprising that this is controversial. We saw in chapter 1 that there are important arguments against the view that moral considerations are ascertained by reason or constructed by reason, and that there is a correlate to this objection with regard to motivation. How can reason, which is a faculty for understanding, also be a faculty with motivational efficacy? Doesn't the "energy" for motivation always have to have a source in desire, concern, interest, or affect in *some* way? Those are the things that *move* us. In deciding how to act we of course employ reason. But reason is not the source of motivation.

Hume famously held that reason on its own does not and cannot have motivational efficacy, and the contrast between his view and Kant's highlights some of the central issues of moral psychology. Hume's claims about motivation were part of his larger view of the limited power of reason in respect to morality. He wrote:

> Since morals, therefore, have an influence on the actions and affections, it follows, that they cannot be deriv'd from reason; and that because reason alone, as we have already prov'd, can never have any such influence. Morals excite passions, and produce or prevent actions. Reason of itself is utterly impotent in this particular.[1]

And:

Actions may be laudable or blameable; but they cannot be reasonable or unreasonable: Laudable or blameable, therefore, are not the same with reasonable and unreasonable. The merit and demerit of actions frequently contradict, and sometimes control our natural propensities. But reason has no such influence. Moral distinctions, therefore, are not the offspring of reason. Reason is wholly inactive, and can never be the source of so active a principle as conscience, or a sense of morals.[2]

Hume interpreted reason's practical employment in predominantly instrumental terms. Reason is used in the service of ends supplied from outside reason, and unless reason is engaged to feeling or desire, it cannot move us to act. The questions of what morality requires and what moves us to do what is required are not answered in terms of reason alone. Reason is not practical in the strong Kantian sense.

Nothing is lost to morality (the Humean will argue) if moral concern and motivation are grounded in human sentiment. Anyway, how could moral considerations motivate unless they engaged agents through feeling and desire? Hume wrote:

It has been observ'd, that reason, in a strict and philosophical sense, can have an influence on our conduct only after two ways: Either when it excites a passion by informing us of the existence of something which is a proper object of it; or when it discovers the connexion of causes and effects, so as to afford us means of exerting any passion.[3]

Reason is not without a role in guiding action, but it functions *only* in conjunction with passion and desire.

Compare that to Kant's view.

Only a rational being has the capacity of acting according to the conception of laws, i.e., according to principles. This capacity is will. Since reason is required for the derivation of actions from laws, will is nothing else than practical reason. If reason infallibly determines the will, the actions which such a being recognizes as objectively necessary are also subjectively necessary. That is, the will is a faculty of choosing only that which reason, independently of inclination, recognizes as practically necessary, i.e., as good.[4]

Thus, reason (as a faculty of volition, as a practical faculty and not just a faculty for understanding) has a direct, essential, action-guiding role. It is because we are rational agents (Kant held) that we are responsive to moral considerations and for that reason moral considerations have authority for us in determining what to do. To the Kantian, the Humean view lacks the resources to account for the way in which moral requirements are categorical. It seems to make them conditional upon feeling or desire – and moral requirements (Kant argued) are not conditional upon *anything*. Morality, Kant thought, is concerned with what is unconditionally required. Any conditioning of a requirement takes the proposed action out of the category of the morally necessary.

Thus, on the Kantian view it is a failure of rationality not to be motivated by moral considerations. Moral requirements are structured by formal considerations of practical reason, and there is no sense in which they are, so to speak, rationally discretionary. Because of how Kant conceived the relation between unconditional value, rationality, and freedom, he held that when we are not motivated by respect for the moral law we forfeit a measure of our agency and autonomy. Those are capacities by virtue of which we are *persons* and not merely *things*, and they are grounded in our ability to think and act according to the conception of principles. Things (non-persons) are governed by causal laws and do not act according to principles and norms of their own making. That is because they lack reason. That is why there can be no moral obligations for them.

Hume held that our commitment to morality was grounded in what he called our "humanity." We have a sensibility such that certain kinds of concerns and considerations are of interest to us. They matter in ways that are enlarged and elaborated as recognizably moral concerns and moral considerations. To not have them would be very strange, and an agent lacking them is a disturbing and alien sort of character. However, it is not clear that the lack of moral concern is indicative of a straightforward failure of rationality. An agent who is morally vacuous and uninterested in moral considerations could still exhibit rationality in his choices and actions. Being moral or being concerned to respond to moral considerations is not an essential feature of practical reason in the Humean view. To the Humean, the Kantian view seems to implausibly overstate the role of reason in action. Still, even according to Hume, it would be a misrepresentation to interpret the view as making morality simply a matter of choice or decision. Some of our deepest and most enduring concerns and interests are not chosen. We find that we have them by nature. That does not mean we are naturally virtuous or vicious or that we have innate moral knowledge. It means that there are susceptibilities, propensities, and modes of concern that are grounded in our human nature. A morally good person is someone in whom those features of human nature have been encouraged and developed in certain ways.

This debate about moral motivation is part of a larger debate about how best to understand human nature, human action, and practical reason. Kant's view is a paradigmatic example of the position that the nature of rational agency is the key to understanding human action and moral motivation. Hume's view is a paradigmatic example of the position that morality is best understood in terms of the way in which we naturally have certain concerns, passions, and desires, and how reason can help to organize and fulfill them. The Humean view is not that the agent thinks to himself, "If I act morally I'll feel better about things and avoid remorse and criticism. Therefore, I will do the right thing." Nor does the agent think, "It is fortunate that I want to do what morality requires, because otherwise there would be nothing at all in favor of doing it, as far as I am concerned." Rather, the agent with good (or at least decent) character recognizes what is morally required and does it because it is important to him and he finds it agreeable to do so. He has stable overall dispositions in favor of doing morally right acts because of the way in which his sensibility has been developed and educated by experience. He has a concern to do the right thing, but it is not a concern grounded in pure practical reason, nor is it grounded in narrow self-interested or prudential reason.

Many philosophers influenced by Hume have held that nothing intrinsic to moral considerations makes responsiveness to them somehow required by rationality. Mackie, for example, argued that it is indeed correct to regard moral judgments as universalizable in the sense that there is no morally relevant difference between persons just because this one is this one, and that one is that one. For whomever one is, there is nothing morally privileged about being the one that you are. However, he also insists on the following.

> But this does not give universalizable maxims any intrinsic, objective, superiority to non-universalizable ones. The institution of morality itself is not thus given any intrinsic authority, nor is the principle that we should use only universalizable maxims to guide conduct thus enabled to command rational assent.[5]

Mackie argued that if one has made a commitment to a certain institution, or if one is concerned to participate in certain practices (such as the institution and practices of morality), then there are certain rational requirements one must meet in order to participate in a genuine fashion. Once you have made the decision to involve yourself, how you are involved is governed by rules that are not simply up to you. However, whether to participate or whether to make the commitment or to have that kind of concern is not itself a demand or command of reason. We might suggest to you reasons for participating, or we might think it odd that you lack the concern to participate, but lacking that concern or opting not to participate is not in its own right indicative of a failure of rationality. The point at issue is whether participation in morality is "mandated" by rationality, or is grounded in a stance or commitment of some kind. On this sort of view it could be appropriate to criticize the agent who did not regard moral considerations as having a very strong claim on him, even as overriding all other considerations, but that would be a criticism from *within* morality. The commitment to morality can be (this view says) full-fledged, but without being a requirement on pain of irrationality.

In recent decades, expressivists have taken over and developed some of the central Humean claims. While for Kant, moral motivation could not come from any subjective or contingent source, there is also the opposing view that moral motivation *must* have such a source. A consideration cannot function as a *practical* reason unless it is responsive to or reflective of some interest or concern the agent has, which is itself not arrived at just on the basis of belief and reasoning. The agent has to *care* about something, and caring ultimately has to do with feeling or desire. It is because moral judgments express attitudes and stances that they have motivational force.

In a recent defense of the Kantian view Christine Korsgaard has argued that a rational agent has a conception of his or her practical identity, a conception supplied by the reasons for action one reflectively endorses. "The reflective structure of human consciousness requires that you identify yourself with some law or principle which will govern your choices. It requires you to be a law to yourself. And that is the source of normativity."[6] Moreover, "Your reasons express your identity, your nature; your obligations spring from what that identity forbids."[7] It is because we are capable of reflecting upon action-guiding considerations, and endorsing some rather than others as principles of the will, that we are aware of and responsive to moral obligations. A rational agent just is an agent who can reflectively assess desires and passions and determine which to endorse and enact, and which to disavow or repudiate as not fitting into one's conception of what there is reason to do. There is a fundamental role for reason because deliberate action is motivated by reflective endorsements of a sort that only rational agents are capable of. This borrows heavily from Kant's conception of rational agency without some of Kant's commitments to the notion of pure practical reason. It is a view in which desires, impulses, and concerns are material for reason to reflect upon and evaluate, but it is through our rationality that we determine what obligates us. Reason has functions that are much more robust than being merely instrumental with respect to action. Obligation is a normative notion, a notion of what we should do or ought to do, not just a notion of what we want to do or feel impelled to do. Moreover, we are capable of recognizing that some principles of action are rational for all agents; they are universalizable. We are capable of recognizing principles of moral rationality. The structure and the force of those principles, their authority as action-guiding, are all based in reason in this Kantian-inspired view.

Virtue and Motivation

While the contrast between the Humean view and the Kantian view is an excellent basis for exploring the respective roles of reason, feeling, and desire in moral motivation, those approaches do not exhaust the topic. For example, Aristotle held a view in which sensibility, desire, and judgment have roles and in which they are aligned (rather than being in conflict) in the well ordered agent. Neither reason alone nor sensibility alone is adequate to explain morally relevant human action. The virtuous person enjoys acting well, finding it naturally pleasing. Given the agent's desires, his conceptions of worth, and the way that he appreciates situations, he is concerned to do what virtue requires because that is what informs his conception of what is good. The virtuous agent is not someone who recognizes what is morally required and then, after considering whether to do it or to follow other desires or interests, decides in favor of morality. He does not have to resolve conflicts between morality and desire, or morality and feeling. This is because the virtuous agent wants to do what he recognizes to be right. Desire and understanding agree in such a way that the agent finds it pleasing to act well.

We are animals and, as such, we are moved by passion and desire;

but we are *rational* animals. Rational animals form conceptions of good and what is worthwhile on the basis of understanding, and they decide what to do on the basis of deliberation that employs that understanding. The involvement of passion and desire does not derationalize action. Aristotle wrote: "Thought by itself, however, moves nothing; what moves us is thought aiming at some goal and concerned with action."[8] And "decision is desire together with reason that aims at some goal. Hence decision requires understanding, and thought and also a state of character, since doing well or badly in action requires both thought and character."[9] It is because we have passions and desires that we move and act at all. However, we are capable of guiding action by a cognitive appreciation of what merits being chosen and being done.

Aristotle says of virtuous agents:

> Hence their life does not need pleasure to be added [to virtuous activity] as some sort of ornament; rather, it has its pleasure within itself. For besides the reasons already given, someone who does not enjoy fine actions is not good; for no one would call him just, e.g., if he did not enjoy doing just actions, or generous if he did not enjoy generous actions, and similarly for the other virtues.[10]

Virtuous agents find virtuous activity naturally pleasing. They act in such a way that they enjoy the goods that are proper to a human being. It is not a struggle for them to be motivated to do what is right (which is not to say that it is easy or fun). Their concern is with *what* virtue requires, not *whether* to do what virtue requires. The virtuous agent, so to speak, loves the right things. This person aims to do fine and just actions and would find it painful not to act virtuously. The agent is engaged with good both cognitively and affectively. The virtuous agent is attached to true values and wants to be so, and experiences regret when he acts badly or succumbs to weakness of will.

Both Plato and Aristotle understood moral excellence in terms of an agent's rationally desiring the good, in spite of the fact that they have different conceptions of the metaphysics of moral value. (You might look at chapter 6 of Book I of the *Nicomachean Ethics* for Aristotle's critique of Plato's conception of the form of the good.) They both maintained that a virtuous agent has a well ordered soul. That is a soul in which reason has authority over desire and passion, so that they aim at their proper objects. They have an important role in action and response (e.g. anger, admiration, gratitude) instead of needing to be repressed, subordinated, or eliminated. Well ordered desires and passions enable the agent to discern what reason understands to be good and help motivate the agent to act accordingly.

It is in each individual's interest to flourish, to live well, and knowledge of the good is necessary in order to do so. Leading a life of virtuous activity is prudent, but not in the "thin" sense that it promotes the self-interest of the agent, enabling him to do or attain what he happens to most strongly desire. Nor is this the kind of prudence exhibited in rational economic behavior (on a prevailing model of what that is). This is prudence in a richer sense, as the virtue of practical wisdom, as action-guiding knowledge of good. Virtuous activity perfects one's nature, and that excellent activity is enjoyed. The virtuous agent's happiness is grounded in his virtuous activity.

It might look as though this view is a combination of Kantian and Humean elements. It assigns an important role to reason, but also to desire and sensibility. To see it as a combination, though, would be a mistake. The Kantian and Humean views are too different to just be combined. As an analogy, consider again the free will and determinism debate. We cannot combine determinism and libertarianism to arrive at compatibilism. After all, the determinist asserts that determinism (the thesis that all events are causally necessitated) is true and the libertarian asserts that it is false. Compatibilism is a third view, not a synthesis of the other two. Similarly, though Plato's and Aristotle's accounts of moral motivation maintain that reason is involved, and so are appetite and passion, they are not combinations of Kantian claims about the efficacy of practical reason and Humean skepticism about practical reason. For Plato and Aristotle, the alignment of desire and sensibility with what reason understands to be good is crucial. The agent has rational desires in the sense that he desires what is proper for a human being. That way of speaking of the integration of reason and desire is not quite at home in either the Humean or Kantian views. For Kant, reason both ascertains what is to be done and motivates action. According to Hume, reason has a role in action only in so far as it is engaged to ends and motives from sources other than reason.

Self-interest and Morality

At some point either in or outside of class you have probably encountered the claim that "everyone is motivated solely by self-interest" or that "whatever people do, and whatever they might say about their motives, they really act only with a view to their own interests." This is a view well worth reflecting on, asking if indeed the evidence supports it. It is certainly not a conceptual or definitional truth that all motives are self-interested. It is not part of the *meaning* of the term "motive" that all motives are self-interested. In addition, it is no better to argue from "every motive is some individual's motive" to "therefore, all motives are self-interested" than it is to argue from "every belief is some subject's belief" to "therefore, all beliefs are subjective." You might consider counterexamples to both claims. You should be able to think of many.

With regard to motives and self-interest, think about the sorts of things friends do for each other and why they do those things. (Think also about the difference between a genuine friend and a friend who is less than a genuine friend.) Consider the kinds of things family members do for each other and why, and the ways people (not all people, to be sure) help others in times of disaster or severe need, or, for that matter, just to be helpful. However, even if it is false that people are only motivated by what they take to be their own self-interest, there remains an important issue concerning the relation of self-interest to morality. Maybe not everything everybody does is self-interested, but it still might be true that the motive to act morally needs to be self-interested if it is to be regular and reliable.

One important strategy concerning self-interest and morality is famously presented in the work of Thomas Hobbes. This strategy engages agents to moral considerations through rational self-interest. There is disagreement over whether to interpret Hobbes's view as "pure" **egoism** but we need not enter that scholarly dispute right here. The point is that one way to explain the motivation to act on moral considerations is by showing that it is in each agent's rational interest to do so. There are gains to self-interest in acting morally, in cooperating with others, making good-faith agreements, regulating one's actions to take into account the responses and desires of others, and so on. In this way, each one of us is best able to secure important benefits to ourselves. (This is why we enter into the social contract.) It is prudent, in our own rational self-interest, to be moral. The risks that come with opting out of, or never entering into, morality are very great. There is a great deal that rational self-interest can say on behalf of morality, and there would not be much to say on behalf of morality if that were not the case.

The view says that it is rational to be moral, not just to *appear* to be moral, or to be moral on just those occasions when it obviously serves our interest. This is not the position that we can suspend or abandon morality when some other course seems to be more in our interest. It is a view about the rationality of being moral in a general, reliable way, not on a case-by-case basis. Self-interest need not be interpreted as ruthless and uncompromising, involving duplicity and fraud whenever one can get away with them. A self-interest rationale for morality can be a rationale for genuine morality, for entering into a set of agreements that minimize our exposure to force and fraud. This is a way of answering the question, "what reason is there to be moral?" which appeals directly to the agent through a concern that he already has in a sustained and effective manner. This is a reason that easily generates a motive to be moral. Many people do a bad job of pursuing their interests (they are impetuous, ill-informed, weak of will, etc.) but self-interest is an abiding concern that everyone has. If moral considerations can be seen to have the appeal of self-interest then the motivational issue would be largely solved, *if* it is true that an attachment to self-interest is essential to moral motivation.

We have already seen that there are views (such as Kant's) that deny this and also maintain that the motive to be moral must be *independent* of self-interest or it will be deeply compromised. Kant thought that self-interest was indeed a powerful motive but that we can be motivated just by the recognition that an action is morally required, without the admixture or assistance of self-interest. He did not argue that we should somehow eliminate self-interest from our practical reasoning, but he did argue that morally worthy action could not be motivated by self-interest.

There are also views that acknowledge that self-interest is a constant and powerful motive but insist that there are other motives as well, such as benevolence and an interest in promoting mutual benefit that play an important role in morality. This is the sort of view we find in Hume and Smith. It seemed plain to them that doing good for others out of feeling for their welfare, out of concern for their good, was a common and potentially powerful motive that could be cultivated and enlarged. In their view, self-interest and concern for others combined to generate and sustain morality. (Their works, coming a century after Hobbes's, reflected assimilation of critiques of Hobbes by their predecessors, people such as Hutcheson, Shaftesbury, Butler, and others. The debate about egoism was especially prominent in the seventeenth and eighteenth centuries and it remains a live philosophical issue. There are interesting historical and philosophical reasons why the issue was front and center then. You might investigate those reasons.)

Hume and Smith belong to a long tradition of British moral theorizing according to which it is *sentiment* that unites us in a common moral world. The required sentiments are present in us as part of our human nature. We find the successes and happiness of others pleasing to us; we are pained by the suffering and misfortune of others; we feel compassion for those who are destitute and wretched; we admire generosity, sacrifice, and public spirit and are often moved to emulate them. These thinkers did not have illusions about how selfless or compassionate people are. They knew that most people are mainly concerned with their own interests. But they also insisted that people are by no means exclusively self-interested and do not want to be. The bases of moral concern and the motive to act on moral considerations were to be found in feeling rather than reason, and that feeling is not narrowly egoistic.

Hume, for example, wrote:

> So far from thinking, that men have no affection for any thing beyond themselves, I am of opinion, that tho' it be rare to meet with one, who loves any single person better than himself; yet 'tis as rare to meet with one, in whom all the kind affections, taken together, do not over-balance all the selfish.[11]

And:

> Have we any difficulty to comprehend the force of humanity and benevolence? Or to conceive, that the very aspect of happiness, joy, prosperity, gives pleasure; that of pain, suffering, sorrow, communicates uneasiness?[12]

Adam Smith wrote:

> It is thus that man, who can subsist only in society, was fitted by nature to that situation for which he was made. All the members of human society stand in need of each others assistance, and are likewise exposed to mutual injuries. Where the necessary assistance is reciprocally afforded from love, from gratitude, from friendship, and esteem, the society flourishes and is happy. All the different members of it are bound together by the agreeable bands of love and affection, and are, as it were, drawn to one common centre of mutual good offices.[13]

Smith did not think that benevolence was the whole of virtue, and like many of the ancients he so much admired, he believed that "the love of what is honourable and noble"[14] was even stronger than the love of mankind. Still, he did not feel that a full-scale argumentative assault on egoism was necessary. Like many other theorists (many, but certainly not all) he believed that it was plain that benevolence or sympathy operated as a motive and that it could be extended and reinforced to strengthen moral concern.

The influence of this tradition can be seen a century later in Mill's thinking. Mill held a hedonist theory of value but, as we have seen, it was not egoistic hedonism. He wrote of the basis of utilitarian morality:

> This firm foundation is that of the social feelings of mankind – the desire to be in unity with our fellow creatures, which is already a powerful principle in human nature, and happily one of those which tend to become stronger, even without express inculcation, from the influences of advancing civilization.[15]

People do not have to be dynamited out of egoism in order to be moral. They do not have to be convinced that morality is in their self-interest in order for moral considerations to have any weight with them, and concern for others is not something that has to extracted from people. That would not *be* concern for others. Mill argued that there is no "inherent necessity that any human being should be a selfish egotist, devoid of every feeling or care but for those which center in his own miserable individuality."[16] People *naturally* have compassion and concern for others. That is part of human sensibility that, of course, can be stunted, hardened, or habituated in ways that cause it to wither. Still, it would be precious to say, "when one acts for the good of another because one wants to, that is actually self-interested because the agent is only doing the action to satisfy his or her own wants." We noted above that this move is either a failed definitional claim ("if P has a desire, that desire must be for something for P") or it is an empirical claim, which in many cases seems to be just plain false. Often, what we want to do is help the other person, relieve suffering, offer our support, and the like, for the sake of other people. It may please us to do so, but that hardly makes it self-interested.

In our discussion of moral motivation we noted that in Aristotle's view reason and desire are aligned in virtuous activity. We also saw that Aristotle held that a virtuous agent leads an excellent, flourishing life. However, the point of being moral is not just to pursue one's own happiness, though virtuous activity is the way to most successfully do so. A flourishing life is one in which excellences of character are most fully actualized. We can come to recognize and appreciate what is good in such a way that we aim at what reason understands to be good and enjoy realizing it in our activities. Again, being good is a good to the agent who is good, but the reasons to be good are not egoistic reasons.

The Platonic view is that the just agent, by being good and not being corrupt in any respect, lives the best, most profitable life, even if the agent experiences suffering of other kinds. Justice is the virtue that correctly orders the soul. The just individual loves what is truly worthy, derives proper pleasures from his activities, and does so in a way that is stable and harmonious. Being just benefits the agent who is just because only reason cares for the whole soul, and when the soul is well ordered it is satisfied as a whole. Plato says, "when the entire soul follows the philosophic part, and there is no civil war in it, each part of it does its own work exclusively and is just, and in particular it enjoys its own pleasures, the best and truest pleasures possible for it."[17] The unjust person is subject to tempests of desire, frustration, and changes of mind about what is worthwhile. Thus, being morally good is the greatest good for the individual, but not in a narrowly egoistic way. In the *Republic*, speaking through Socrates, Plato says that in the just person "his entire soul settles into its best nature, acquires moderation, justice, and reason, and attains a more valuable state than that of having a fine, strong healthy body."[18] To do anything disgraceful or unjust, even to escape punishment, will make a man worse by corrupting him. Justice is more profitable than injustice, and virtue is in one's interest in the deepest and most enduring way.

According to both Plato and Aristotle virtuous activity is in the best interest of the individual because excellent activity is enjoyed in a distinctively rich and stable way, and the agent appreciates the true worth of his activities. This is hardly a conception of flourishing or excellence that invites interpretation in a narrowly egoistic way. (You might compare Plato's and Aristotle's views to Hobbes's view. Doing so will supply you with conceptual resources and insights concerning fundamental debates about how to understand the relations between reason, desire, and good.)

Even though we have raised some important objections to a narrow self-interest model of moral motivation, the egoist plays an important role in the debate about motivation. That role is analogous to the one the skeptic plays with respect to knowledge. The skeptic holds that some type of knowledge-claim is vulnerable to doubt and cannot be adequately justified. Skeptics also insist that in order to be intellectually responsible we must meet skeptical challenges and cannot just put them aside.

Some philosophers examining the question of knowledge argue that many of the skeptic's challenges are not altogether genuine. It may be that we do not have to meet and defeat skeptical hypotheses. This is especially the case with regard to "global" skepticism, the denial that any of our knowledge claims are (or even can be) completely justified. It is one thing to raise challenges to this or that specific claim; perhaps the conditions of observation were poor, or the agent was suffering from exhaustion. It is indeed necessary to be able to respond to many kinds of specific challenges motivated by specific doubts. But a number of influential philosophers, including Thomas Reid, G. E. Moore, Ludwig Wittgenstein, and Roderick Chisholm, have argued (in different ways) that global skeptical challenges are less threatening than they claim to be.

Their point is that the acceptability of knowledge claims does not require an antecedent argument that proves that knowledge or certainty is possible. Rather, there are certain kinds of claims that recognizably count as knowledge, *unless we have a special reason to doubt them.* These approaches typically try to show that while there often are reasons to doubt knowledge claims, there is not a completely general skeptical challenge to knowledge (such as a doubt that our memory and sensory and reasoning capacities are reliable) that must be eliminated before we are in a position to make specific knowledge claims. The philosophers mentioned give different accounts of why and how this is so – they do not just dogmatically assert that we have knowledge. What they share is the conviction that the skeptic is insisting on an implausibly and unnecessarily high standard of justification for knowledge claims.

In the moral context, the egoist might argue that any claim that an action was motivated by considerations other than self-interest is open to challenge. At some level, whether the agent is aware of it or not, the decisive motivating consideration is self-interest. Our most confident knowledge claims (says the skeptic) are vulnerable to doubt. Similarly, the most altruistic or unselfish actions can be interpreted (says the egoist) as actually due to self-interest. There's the crux of the matter: they *can* be interpreted that way. But do we have good reason for thinking such an interpretation is *true*? Perhaps many kinds of knowledge claims are innocent unless there is a special reason to find them suspect or guilty. Perhaps actions that do not appear to be motivated by self-interest really are not. Again, consider the things parents and children do for each other, and the ways friends enjoy each other's successes. Also, we are sometimes kind and generous to strangers just because we think it is a good idea, and so forth. Should we think that all such claims are self-serving, or misrepresentations, or based upon illusion or other errors? Maybe what looks like the explanation really *is* the explanation. Perhaps in the context of knowledge we do not have to prove that highly general skeptical hypotheses are false, and perhaps here we do not have to argumentatively prove that egoist hypotheses are false.

What about Luck?

Whatever our account of moral value and moral motivation, we can still ask, "to what extent is the moral value of our actions *up to us*?" To what extent is the moral worth of what we do a matter of *what we do* in the sense that we have control over our acts and their outcomes? These are questions concerning moral luck, and the ways it presents important challenges to moral thought and moral theory. They raise difficulties about the stability and coherence of moral judgment. This is because there are many factors we do not control but which seem to make a difference to the moral significance of our actions.

A direct route into the significance of this issue is through Kant's theorizing. Kant's emphasis on the way in which moral value is unconditioned and the way in which moral value resides entirely in the character of rational volition is indicative of his concern to make morality as far as possible immune to luck. He held that as free agents, we are the sole authors of the moral worth of our actions. The moral worth of our actions is "up to" us, and not determined by factors we do not or cannot control. *We* invest actions with moral worth by the manner in which we exert ourselves as voluntary, rational agents. If that were not the case, we could still talk of actions and situations as being better or worse, as pleasing or welcome, or as undesirable or harmful. But we could not find in them distinctively *moral* worth. There would be dimensions across which actions and situations could be evaluated but they would not include the distinctively moral dimension.

That dimension, Kant argued, concerns rational volition alone. Why should this be? Why is it not enough that there is a difference between good states of affairs and bad states of affairs? To answer these questions, consider the difference between humans and other creatures. Many non-human animals experience fear, pleasure, anxiety, pain, distress, comfort, and so forth. There are dimensions across which we can plausibly say that their lives are going well or badly. Kant would argue that because they are not capable of authoring their actions according to rational principles, they are not moral agents. There is pleasure and suffering that is independent of morality, and there are non-moral kinds of value. But moral value is essentially a matter of what an agent knowingly, intentionally undertakes for its own sake, because it is right – whatever the fate of that action, given the way of the world. Only the acts of rational agents can have moral worth and the value of those acts is not vulnerable to luck.

In the present context luck is not randomness or chance, but all those things over which we do not have effective control through our own volition. Those include many of the consequences of our actions, many of the circumstances in which we find ourselves, and even features of our characters, such as natural propensities and temperament. The view that the morality of an action concerns only rational volition and does not involve luck is an attempt to separate out the sphere of rational agency (and its special value) from all else. Bernard Williams characterized the view (of which he is quite critical) as follows: "Such a conception has an ultimate form of justice at its heart, and that is its allure. Kantianism is only superficially repulsive – despite appearances, it offers an inducement, solace to a sense of the world's unfairness."[19] Should things turn out badly because of the way of the world, that is unfortunate, but not a basis of moral criticism of us, if we did the right thing, or tried to do so. Moral worth is unaffected by the course of things governed by anything other than the exercise of rational agency. This is part of Kant's rejection of **consequentialism**. (A consequentialist maintains that acts are to be morally evaluated on the basis of what they bring about – what difference they make – rather than in terms of motive or the character of the agent. We will explore this much more fully in the next chapter.) Kant argued that moral worth "can lie nowhere else than in the principle of the will, irrespective of the ends which can be realized by such action."[20]

One way in which the Kantian view is reflected in many people's thinking is in the notion that a morally sound motive or intention morally vindicates an act that may otherwise be evaluated negatively. Moral sincerity, integrity, and resolve often seem enough to save moral worth, even if the outcome or the repercussions are regrettable or even tragic. Indeed, tragedy is often a feature of our lives. Sometimes all of the realistic options are imperfect, or no matter what effort we make or how much integrity we exhibit, the result is harm to someone who does not deserve it. The world can be a hard and unhappy place despite our best efforts and we do not have sovereignty over what happens in it. However, if our own contribution is that we undertake to do the right thing because it is right, we can (Kant thought) separate out the moral worth of our agency from everything else. We have power over whether we do the right thing. Kant thought that unless this is true, morality would be altogether undone. There can only be morality if there is rational autonomy. Having rational autonomy does not mean that our volitions can always be efficacious but it does mean that what we will is entirely up to us, and that is the source of moral value. In Kant's theory moral value is not "at risk" on account of the way of the world. The moral worth of actions is not determined by their success or failure at bringing about an end or a certain kind of state of affairs.

For Mill, moral luck was not a concern in the same way. The utilitarian is interested in bringing about the best state of affairs, and the question of whether we are sole authors of our actions and motives is not essential to that. (In the way Mill uses the terms, "motive" refers to what moves you to act, and "intention" refers to that which you undertake to bring about. Five different people might share the intention to assassinate the head of the secret police, but they might each have their own distinct motives. One is motivated by political ideology, another is a paid hit-man motivated by greed, and so forth.) Mill distinguished between the rightness of an action and the worth of an agent, noting that motive has a bearing on the latter rather than on the former. He wrote:

> The morality of the action depends entirely upon the intention – that is, upon what the agent wills to do. But the motive, that is, the feeling which makes him will so to do, if it makes no difference to the act, makes none in the morality: though it makes a great difference in our moral estimation of the agent, especially if it indicates a good or bad habitual disposition – a bent of character from which useful, or from which hurtful actions are likely to arise.[21]

Mill did not insist on the purity of motive essential to Kant's moral theory, nor did he argue that our intentions must be free of causal influences. Morality concerns what we try to bring about, not whether we are autonomous in our exercise of agency.

We should note, though, that intentions too are subject to moral luck in a couple of important ways. One is that there is a role for luck in how we have been influenced, socialized, and educated. Our characteristic patterns of intention and action depend upon a great many factors we do not control and may not even be aware of. Moreover, there is a measure of moral luck with regard to what results from acting on our intentions. How things "turn out" is subject to luck in many ways. As Thomas Nagel observes, "In many cases of difficult choice the outcome cannot be foreseen with certainty. One kind of assessment of the choice is possible in advance, but another kind must await the outcome, because the outcome determines what has been done."[22] We are often held responsible for how things "turn out" even though there is a substantial measure of luck involved. Additionally, we often take credit for how things "turn out" even though luck is involved. We simply do not control the whole course of our actions and what they result in. As Nagel points out, what one *did* often depends upon outcome.

The fact that Mill did not explicitly discuss moral luck does not show that it is not an issue for a consequentialist. One way in which moral luck is acknowledged by consequentialists is in distinguishing between the objective rightness of actions (bringing about the best state of affairs) and the subjective rightness of actions (acting on intentions to do the best thing, given one's knowledge and capabilities). We are to do our best at bringing about certain ends, and we need to act on our best understanding of the way of the world. But we cannot perfectly predict or control the course of events even when we are informed and carefully deliberate in our choice of actions. The issue of moral luck cannot be escaped by any moral theory, though different theories are subject to its pressures in different ways. Even the Kantian theory feels the pressure in that the notion of pure rational agency, independent of the influences of character, experience, and prior choices, is a problematic notion. That agent begins to look more and more like a rational "someone" who is not anyone in particular – or rather, there is no one for that rational "someone" to be. Is that the sort of agent who *could* choose and direct action? In making rational agency immune to luck, Kant may have rendered it almost unrecognizable as the agent who makes choices, has concerns, and aspires to realize certain values and ends.

Luck is also an issue for virtue-centered moral theories because of the central role of character and the ways in which early stages of formation of character are very substantially subject to influences we do not control. We do not (especially as young people) have control over the people we are surrounded by and what sort of influence over us they have. Aristotle agreed with Plato that one's early moral education, before one is able to make one's own judgments and fashion one's own policies of reasoning, is extremely important. "It is not unimportant, then, to acquire one sort of habit or another, right from our youth; rather, it is very important, indeed all-important."[23] "Hence we need to have had the appropriate upbringing – right from early youth, as Plato says – to make us find enjoyment or pain in the right things; for this is the correct education."[24] We are individually responsible for the mature characters we develop, but we are dependent upon others for early guidance. (See, in particular, Book 3 of *Nicomachean Ethics* for Aristotle's argument that we are responsible for our characters.)

It is a matter of luck whether we are born into wealth or poverty, or among people who care about education and culture or prefer idle or vulgar amusements. It is also a matter of luck whether by natural temperament we are more or less able to acquire the virtues. Some people have even dispositions and moderate appetites – and others do not. Some people are naturally timid and others are not. And so forth. "For each of us seems to possess his type of character to some extent by nature, since we are just, brave, prone to temperance, or have another feature, immediately from birth."[25] In addition, the circumstances and challenges we face involve luck. Maybe our courage will never be tested in certain ways. It is easy to say what someone else should have done when we ourselves have never faced such circumstances. Maybe an agent's predicament is desperate and frightening. How are we to evaluate the behavior of people in concentration camps, or in the aftermath of war or a natural disaster that makes life precarious? What sorts of standards of responsibility, what sorts of norms of behavior reasonably and appropriately apply in such cases? There may be a sense in which we are confident about what one should do in the situation, but what is the ground for our confidence that *we* could do it? Is the ability or inability to do it traceable to luck? Even if it is true that in important respects we are responsible for our actions and our states of character, we are not literally "self-made," and the "materials" of character and the influences at work on the shaping of it are, to a large extent, matters of luck.

While Aristotle saw that there is an important role for luck in our lives, he argued that whether we lead excellent and happy lives is voluntary.

> But surely it is quite wrong to be guided by someone's fortunes. For his doing well or badly does not rest on them; though a human life, as we said, needs these added, it is the activities expressing virtue that control happiness, and the contrary activities that control its contrary.[26]

Aristotle held that virtue, "the soul's activity that expresses reason",[27] is what most fundamentally makes for an excellent life and the actualization of human good. What is best for us is something that is accessible to us through our own causality, though he acknowledged that, "many strokes of good fortune will make it [one's life] more blessed".[28] Moreover, "happiness evidently also needs external goods to be added [to the activity], as we said, since we cannot, or cannot easily, do fine actions if we lack the resources."[29] External goods such as friends, material means, and a well ordered political community in which to live are all needed. If you are to do fine things you need the resources to do them, and if you are to develop the virtues to a high degree there are enabling conditions, which are not controlled by your own choices and actions.

Everyone's life is shot through with luck, some of it good, some of it bad. Do those with good luck morally "owe" more to others? Is it appropriate to *expect* them to be virtuous because they have had the advantages of good luck? We might think that if someone is intelligent, capable, and skilled then that person's opportunities and rewards should reflect that. Those who can run fastest should be rewarded for "winning the race," so to speak, and we should give tools to those who can make best use of them. On the other hand, it may also seem that because they are already advantaged by luck, they owe more rather than deserve more. Instead of the rule being "the best deserve the most," perhaps it should be "it is incumbent upon the best to do the most." Questions about what people deserve raise the issue of moral luck in complex and acute ways.

Issues coming under the heading "moral luck" have a bearing on several dimensions of moral experience and judgment. There are questions of luck concerning the relations between motives, intentions, and outcomes. To what extent should success in one's undertakings be relevant to the evaluation of the attempt? If the poison was too weak and the victim did not die, is the poisoning a lesser crime than an attempt at murder that succeeds? There are issues of luck concerning the extent to which we are responsible for our actions and for the values that we endorse. There are issues of luck concerning whether we are able to lead happy and flourishing lives. There isn't some single question of moral luck. Rather, when we are talking about moral luck, we are talking about all the ways in which what we do not and cannot control makes a difference to morality. And there are many such ways.

Here are some questions that might help guide reflection on moral luck. It would be a good exercise to try to think of illustrations of these concerns. It should not be difficult to think of actual cases from your own experience.

1   If one person attempts to perform a right action but fails (e.g. the person he was trying to aid suffocated from smoke before the rescuer could get him out of the burning building) and another person tries and succeeds, are the actions morally equivalent?

2   If, through no fault or negligence of your own, you lose control of your car on an icy road and severely injure someone, is it appropriate to experience any sort of moral regret or remorse? (Or should one just feel that this was unfortunate, and not also feel moral responsibility or regret of any kind?)

3   If two people are equally careless, and one person's carelessness leads to injury or loss while the other person's carelessness does not, should they be subject to the same sort and degree of moral criticism? How does this case differ from the case in (1)?

4   Do evil intentions and designs merit moral blameworthiness even if they are never translated into action?

5   Do virtuous intentions and motives merit moral praise even if the attempt to enact them fails, or actually worsens a situation?

6   Think about what you most want out of life or what would be most fulfilling to you. To what extent does it seem to you that luck is, has been, or could be involved in shaping or realizing those aspirations and projects?

Are Moral Considerations Overriding?

What are the proper limits of the claims of morality? This question concerns the way in which moral considerations fit into practical reasoning overall and the place of morality in a life overall. This is not simply a question of the relation between self-interest and morality. We have many kinds of concerns and there are considerations of value that are not straightforwardly either moral or self-interested. People have many types of interest, affiliation, and involvement that matter to them in diverse ways and answer to different needs and aspirations. Think about the various ways in which work, leisure, friendships, family life, participation in groups, organizations, and institutions matter to a life. Our issue is whether all other ends and concerns are properly subordinated to moral requirements and whether moral impartiality overrides all personal and partial interests and commitments.

One important view is that while there is, of course, room in our lives for personal, subjective interests, ends, and attachments, moral rationality has a privileged position and a privileged claim on us. For example, both the utilitarian and Kantian approaches to morality seem to capture something that resonates deeply with many people. The utilitarian approach requires that we put the promotion of impartial good first. The Kantian approach requires that we put moral principle ahead of our own interests and concerns. Doing so is a way of respecting ourselves and others as rational agents. These conceptions appear to answer the question, "how much of myself or my life am I obligated to give over to moral requirements?" with "all of it," or at least "impartial moral requirements always override other action-guiding considerations." There is a distinctively moral perspective on our actions and we are to adopt that perspective as a fundamental measure of what to do. Moral considerations reflect an ideal that takes priority over other kinds of value.

Bernard Williams, a critic of both Kantian and utilitarian moral theories, writes of Kantian morality:

> The moral point of view is specially characterized by its impartiality and its indifference to any particular relations to particular persons, and that moral thought requires abstraction from particular circumstances and particular characteristics of the parties, including the agent, except in so far as these can be treated as universal features of any morally similar situation.[30]

Similarly, "As a Utilitarian agent, I am just the representative of the satisfaction system who happens to be near certain causal levers at a certain time."[31] Thus, utilitarianism is "basically indifferent to the separateness of those who have the satisfactions."[32] Williams believes both approaches misrepresent agents, their reasons, and their relations with others. They fail to properly appreciate the ways in which quite individual, personal concerns, attachments, and perspectives are ineliminable and fundamental aspects of our lives.

First, is impartiality a requirement of morality in such a way that it always overrides all partial concerns? Does it always override concern for those near to us, dear to us, those with whom we are involved in certain particular ways and for whom we have quite specific feelings and cares? For example, we might think that given our friendship with someone it is appropriate that we should have special concern for that person's well-being and interests even when we are able to do more for others.

In one respect, impartiality appears uncontroversial and unproblematic. No one's moral status is higher or lower than anyone else's. Each person counts for one and no one counts for more than one. However, regarding each person as having the same moral status does not necessarily require that we show no partiality. Couldn't people live morally decent lives in which they did not harm others, treated people fairly, showed some measure of compassion and benevolence, and also focused their lives on their own concerns and the people especially important in their lives? These are not agents who are self-centered or inconsiderate of the interests of others. They recognize the weight and authority of moral considerations, and recognize that there is no moral privilege in being *this one*, for whomever one happens to be, but do not see all questions of value or all reasons for action from a standpoint that demotes interests and relations that are essentially partial.

Is it morally suspect to devote more attention and effort to those close to us – when this is not just because we can be more effective in that way than by helping those far away? Consider flood victims in your state or your country, and flood victims in a distant country. Does morality require that we attend to their needs impartially? Taking morality seriously is not the same thing as regarding impartial moral considerations as automatically overriding all other considerations. We need to be careful here. The point is not that it may be permissible to be less than "fully" moral (whatever one might mean by that). We are not suggesting that the demands of morality are to be relaxed, but that they are susceptible to being overstated. The point is that it is debatable whether being moral requires "blanket," undifferentiated impartiality.

David Hume wrote: "It is wisely ordained by nature, that private connexions should commonly prevail over universal views and considerations; otherwise our affections and actions would be dissipated and lost, for want of a proper limited object."[33] And Adam Smith wrote:

> That wisdom which contrived the system of human affections, as well as that of every other part of nature, seems to have judged that the interest of the great society of mankind would be best promoted by directing the principal attention of each individual to that particular portion of it, which was most within the sphere both of his abilities and of his understanding.[34]

Neither Hume nor Smith was attempting to shrink the significance of impartiality in morality. They are noting that, as a matter of fact, moral concern is most effective and most fully engaged in ways that are responsive to differences in our relations with people. Of course we give to those who are near and dear to us a distinctive kind of attention. Complete impartiality would be almost like a kind of indifference, not in the sense that we would have no moral concern, but in the sense that we would have no *special* kind of concern for people who occupy especially important places in our lives.

There may be a way to fully register the significance of impartiality to morality without leveling the differences in concern and involvement that are inevitable in our lives. What needs to be explicated is *how* this is not a contraction of moral attention but an appropriate manner of focusing and calibrating it. That is a complex and difficult task, but it seems to be unavoidable. Again, even if there are good reasons for thinking that morality does not altogether take over practical reason and automatically supersede all other value, it is not a license to regard moral considerations in a discretionary way. Instead, it raises difficult questions of just how morality fits into a human life and just how its ideals and demands are related to other possible ideals and demands. Consider also that while it is important to treat our friends and members of our families morally, do we do the things we do for them for mainly *moral* reasons? Is that what the best friendships are like? In certain ways, that seems to be a serious distortion.

A related concern is this; does morality make a claim on our whole selves in the respect that moral excellence is the most important and valuable human excellence? There are many kinds of human excellence, and cultivating and enjoying them can mean that less time, effort, and energy is deployed in pursuing distinctively moral purposes and activities. We could always be more morally ambitious or singleminded, and if morality's imperatives overrule all other demands and interests, then perhaps we should mobilize our talents and abilities in the service of it. Susan Wolf, in a discussion of "moral saints" (people who put morality ahead of all other values and ideals), has put the point this way:

> The moral saint, then, may, by happy accident, find himself with nonmoral virtues on which he can capitalize morally or which make psychological demands to which he has no choice but to attend. The point is that, for a moral saint, the existence of these interests and skills can be given at best the status of happy accidents – they cannot be encouraged for their own sakes as distinct, independent aspects of the realization of human good.[35]

The moral saint not only looks at matters impartially but also makes moral excellence the dominating ideal of his life. He does not regard non-moral excellences and values as having great weight in leading an excellent life. He sees excellence primarily or exclusively in moral terms, and so he is rigorously dedicated to having moral considerations control his perspective and his reasoning.

We need to think carefully about what this would mean for personal development, personal relationships, and the ways in which a life can and cannot be fulfilling. There are types of personal excellence that are non-moral, which we value and appreciate a great deal in ourselves and in others. Think about artistic and literary talent, wit, humor, all variety of skills and types of knowledge, and so forth. There are types of resourcefulness, competence, and sensitivity that are non-moral but still highly valued and admired. Think of the person who is especially wonderful with young children, or the person who always makes a social situation relaxed and pleasant. It would be almost perverse to translate those virtues into terms of, say, utility or duty. That is not the basis of valuing them. We value these characteristics independently of whether they are in the service of overall utility or moral duty or are motivated by distinctively moral concern. To be sure, when these characteristics are exhibited and exercised in morally suspect ways their value is tarnished or undermined. Wit that is always at someone else's expense is like that. Or, when a person singlemindedly pursues a certain goal (their business, art, sport, or what have you) in such a way that others are hurt or neglected, we wonder if the moral cost diminishes the accomplishment. It still may be a marvelous and admirable accomplishment, but its value cannot be wholly separated from the moral dimensions of the activity and character that achieved it. But moral value is not the only kind of value and moral goodness or excellence is not the only kind of goodness or excellence. Here is a place where we can see the attraction which many find in Aristotle's view. He did not separate out a distinct, well defined sphere of practical reasoning that was exclusively concerned with moral obligations. Having and exercising the virtues is part of living well and being an excellent person overall, and that kind of excellence extends well beyond responsiveness to a narrow construal of moral requirements and encompasses all aspects of the agent's character, concerns, and activities. Instead of making moral concern the dominant concern of the agent, Aristotle included what we would recognize as moral concern in his conception of excellent activity and an excellent life.

Questions about the relations between different values are some of the key questions about how to carry on the business of living in a world in which there are so many different things to care about, take interest in, and pursue. They are unavoidable questions for any reflective person. We not only have to make judgments and commitments concerning what values to enact and what ideals to pursue, we must also confront the question of how different kinds of value fit together in a life. At the very same time, these concerns are among the grand questions of philosophy and the everyday details of the business of living.

Where Now?

The way in which moral theorizing handles issues of moral psychology is crucial. We can hardly make progress in thinking and arguing about moral issues except through articulation and examination of claims and commitments that belong to metaethics and to moral psychology. With the resources now at our disposal we are well positioned to look at some of the most important forms of moral theory. We will explore different conceptions of the source or locus of moral value and the difference made by those conceptions to the form of moral theory. Is moral value a matter of the consequences of actions, or the agent's motive, or the agent's character, or something else? There are diverse views of the character of moral considerations and how they figure in moral reasoning. One of the key differences between moral theories is in what they take to be the focus of moral attention. Given a view of what is morally relevant, we can fashion an account of what moral reasoning is about and what it is responsive to. The results of these different views are reflected in the form of moral theory. That is what we turn to now.

Questions for Discussion and Reflection

1   Moral luck seems to be present in our actions and our lives in a number of ways. Is there one specific way in which it seems to be especially important? In what ways, if any, does luck raise serious difficulties for the evaluation of agents and actions?

2   To what extent is acting morally required by rationality? Could an agent be rational but unconcerned with morality, or reject its claims? Is that only a moral defect or also a defect in reason?

3   Many kinds of reasons have been offered for the conclusion that agents are not responsible for their characters. If those are good reasons and if character has an important role in moral judgment and motivation, does that mean that we should think that agents are not responsible for their motives and their actions?

4   Explain the notion of self-interest and explicate the distinction (if there is one) between real and perceived self-interest, and its relevance to moral theory.

5   What are the main connections between pleasure, moral value, and happiness? In what ways are any of those to be interpreted in terms of the others?

6   Is it possible to articulate a general answer to the question of what is the proper place of moral value and moral ideals in a human life? Are there kinds of human excellence that can be more important than moral excellence? In what ways should moral considerations shape or limit our aspirations and the central projects of our lives?

Thinkers and Their Works, and Further Reading

Aristotle: *Nicomachean Ethics*
Roderick Chisholm: *Theory of Knowledge*; *Perceiving: A Philosophical Study*
Philippa Foot: *Virtues and Vices*
David Hume: *A Treatise of Human Nature*; *An Enquiry Concerning the Principles of Morals*
Immanuel Kant: *Foundations of the Metaphysics of Morals*; *Religion within the Limits of Reason Alone*; *The Doctrine of Virtue*
Christine Korsgaard: *The Sources of Normativity*; "Skepticism about Practical Reason"
John Mackie: *Ethics: Inventing Right and Wrong*
John McDowell: "Projection and Truth in Ethics"; "Are Moral Requirements Hypothetical Imperatives?"
J. S. Mill: *Utilitarianism*
G. E. Moore: *Principia Ethica*
Thomas Nagel: *Mortal Questions*; *The Possibility of Altruism*
Plato: *Republic*; *Gorgias*; *Laws*
Thomas Reid: *Essays on the Active Powers*
Adam Smith: *The Theory of Moral Sentiments*
Bernard Williams: *Ethics and the Limits of Philosophy*; *Moral Luck*
Ludwig Wittgenstein: *On Certainty*; *Philosophical Investigations*
Susan Wolf: "Moral Saints"

Notes

1   David Hume, *A Treatise of Human Nature*, ed. L. A. Selby-Bigge (Oxford: Oxford University Press, 1978), p. 457.
2   Ibid., p. 458.
3   Ibid., p. 459.
4   Immanuel Kant, *Foundations of the Metaphysics of Morals* (Indianapolis: Bobbs-Merrill, 1976), p. 29.
5   John Mackie, *Ethics: Inventing Right and Wrong* (Harmondsworth: Penguin, 1977), pp. 98–9.
6   Christine Korsgaard, *The Sources of Normativity* (Cambridge: Cambridge University Press, 1997), pp. 103–4.
7   Ibid., p. 101.
8   Aristotle, *Nicomachean Ethics*, trans. Terence Irwin (Indianapolis: Hackett Publishing Company, 1985), 1139a, 35–1139b, 1.

9   Ibid., 1139a, 33–5.
10 Ibid., 1099a, 16–20.
11 Hume, *A Treatise of Human Nature*, p. 487.
12 David Hume, *An Enquiry Concerning the Principles of Morals*, ed. L. A. Selby-Bigge (Oxford: Clarendon Press, 1975), p. 220.
13 Adam Smith, *The Theory of Moral Sentiments*, ed. D. D. Raphael and A. L. MacFie (Indianapolis: Liberty Fund, 1984), p. 85.
14 Ibid., p. 137.
15 J. S. Mill, *Utilitarianism* (Indianapolis: Hackett Publishing Company, 1979), pp. 30–1.
16 Ibid., p. 14.
17 Plato, *Republic*, trans. G. M. A. Grube (Indianapolis: Hackett Publishing Company, 1992), 586e, 258.
18 Ibid., p. 263.
19 Bernard Williams, "Moral Luck," in *Moral Luck* (Cambridge: Cambridge University Press, 1981), p. 21.
20 Kant, *Foundations of the Metaphysics of Morals*, p. 16.
21 Mill, *Utilitarianism*, p. 18.
22 Thomas Nagel, "Moral Luck," in *Mortal Questions* (New York: Cambridge University Press, 1985), p. 30.
23 Aristotle, *Nicomachean Ethics*, 1103b, 24–5.
24 Ibid., 1104b, 11–13.
25 Ibid., 1144b, 4–5.
26 Ibid., 1100b, 8–11.
27 Ibid., 1098a, 7.
28 Ibid., 1100b, 25.
29 Ibid., 1099a, 34–5.
30 Williams, "Persons, Character and Morality," in *Moral Luck*, p. 2.
31 Ibid., p. 4.
32 Ibid., p. 3.
33 Hume, *An Enquiry Concerning the Principles of Morals*, p. 229.
34 Smith, *The Theory of Moral Sentiments*, p. 229.
35 Susan Wolf, "Moral Saints," *Journal of Philosophy*, 79, 8 (1972), p. 425.

3 Forms of Moral Theory

When we attend to the morally relevant features of an action or situation, what sorts of considerations should we take into account? What is the primary focus of concern in moral evaluation? Where is moral value "located" or from what is it derived? Reflection on our own moral experience may reveal a number of different answers to these questions. We might look for moral significance in agents' motives or in the consequences of their actions. We might find it in the character of the agent. Perhaps the agent was courageous and fair even though his action did not have a welcome result. How, then, do we assess the moral worth of the act? (Recall the issue of moral luck.) Is an act that was motivated in a morally suspect way a bad act for that reason alone, even if it had welcome consequences? Our entry into these issues will be through some fairly non-controversial moral claims. By reflecting on them we will be able to see how moral attention can be drawn to various places and we will see what difference that makes to the overall character of moral thought and judgment.

Maybe not everyone agrees on the following claims, but they are undoubtedly widely shared. (a) Lying (in most cases, if not every case) is wrong. (b) Courage is a virtue. (c) It is wrong to harm others for pleasure. (d) It is wrong to knowingly and deliberately harm the innocent. (e) A society in which benefits and burdens are allocated in a completely haphazard or arbitrary way is unjust. (f) Benevolence is morally admirable.

There is a good chance that you accept all or most of those claims. Is there a general strategy of moral thought that connects them in a systematic way? Do they share a common basis? How would they fit into a moral *theory*, rather than just being a collection of beliefs and convictions?

The first thing we should note is that even if we agree that those are correct moral claims, they are claims about different *kinds* of things. The claim about lying is a claim about an action-type. The claim about courage is a claim about a characteristic. Of course, we are interested in the characteristic because of how it is related to action, but in making the claim we are evaluating a state of character, not any particular actions. (We might have reason to morally evaluate characteristics independently of evaluating actions. Later, we will see why this was important to Mill, for example.) The claim about the allocation of benefits and burdens is a claim about the principles of social and economic arrangement. The claim about benevolence is a claim about the moral quality of a motive. And so forth. The list could easily be made longer, and the types of moral considerations, or the objects of moral judgment, could be multiplied.

There appear to be different sorts of objects of moral evaluation and different kinds of considerations that we take into account morally. It may be perfectly all right to acknowledge different grounds or loci of moral value, but it is important to be clear about them. It is especially important to be clear about what sorts of relations they have to each other, and whether one or another has priority or special weight. That makes a crucial difference to what kinds of considerations count as moral reasons and how those reasons figure in the structure of moral thought.

Consequentialism

One approach that has been particularly influential during the past century and a half is *consequentialism*. This is the view that value resides in certain kinds of states of affairs. What is of primary moral importance about an action (or a practice) is what it brings about. To put it simply, the consequentialist maintains that what morally matters about an action is what causal difference it makes, or what it can be expected to bring about. (Some theorists distinguish between what the act in fact brings about and what it is expected to bring about. This allows for the fact that we never have certain and complete knowledge of the consequences of actions. We cannot reasonably expect people to do what is objectively best if we cannot expect them to have complete knowledge. But we can expect them to act on the information they have concerning what would be best.) When we morally evaluate and when we deliberate about what to do, what we look to is the overall difference that is made (or tends to be made) to the state of the world by the act (or type of act) in question.[1] Does truth-telling tend to have better consequences than dishonesty? Are we more likely to achieve a better overall state of affairs by decriminalizing drug use or by carefully limiting it and imposing criminal sanctions on drug possession and use? Is the world overall a better place if we permit active euthanasia? Is it better if we permit and protect private property? What are the comparative consequences of a requirement that we take into account the needs of future generations versus looking after our own needs and concerns? These are examples of the consequentialist mode of thought. The criterion of rightness is specified in terms of what an action brings (or is expected to bring) about.

Different versions of consequentialism involve different conceptions of just what it is about states of affairs that is significant for moral thought. Mill famously held that it was "the influence of actions on happiness"[2] that was most important. He wrote:

> We have now, then, an answer to the question, of what sort of proof the principle of utility is susceptible. If the opinion which I have now stated is psychologically true − if human nature is so constituted as to desire nothing which is not either a part of happiness or a means of happiness − we can have no other proof, and we require no other, that these are the only things desirable. If so, happiness is the sole end of human action, and the promotion of it the test by which to judge of all human conduct; from whence it follows that it must be the criterion of morality, since a part is included in the whole.[3]

Earlier in the same work he had written:

> The creed which accepts as the foundation of morals "utility" or the "greatest happiness principle" holds that actions are right in proportion as they tend to promote happiness; wrong as they tend to produce the reverse of happiness. By happiness is intended pleasure and the absence of pain; by unhappiness, pain and the privation of pleasure.[4]

Mill thought that it was of the first importance to be clear about the criterion of right and wrong, and he believed that he had identified that criterion and that it could be formulated simply. Of course, *apply-ing* it is not always easy, but the crucial issue, he thought, was to have a single, completely general criterion for moral evaluation. As he said, "difference of opinion on moral questions was not first introduced into the world by utilitarianism, while that doctrine does supply, if not always an easy, at all events a tangible and intelligible, mode of decid-ing such differences."[5] If we have a criterion of right and wrong, then we can determine what are our duties in a clear and systematic man-ner and we can resolve moral perplexity by careful application of that criterion. The principle of utility does not itself tell us what to do, and is not intended to. Careful thought and judgment are needed for that. The principle of utility supplies a general criterion of what makes actions right actions.

Not all consequentialists agree with Mill about just what property of states of affairs is morally most important. Moore, for example, was a consequentialist but not a hedonistic utilitarian. What we need to note here is that consequentialism is a certain type of approach to moral theorizing, with a criterion for what sorts of considerations are to be taken into account in moral reasoning. The consequentialist argues that what is at issue is the overall state of the world. Is action A likely to bring about a better state of affairs than action B? If it is, then action A is what morality requires.

We cannot take into account *all* of the probable consequences of an action or a practice because of lack of information, limited ability to interpret information, and lack of time. If we tried to do that, we would never act. We have to rely on prior experience and on know-ledge accumulated by others. It is on that basis that we know that, in general, it is morally right to be honest, to make promises in good faith, to help those in distress, to only punish those we have good reason to believe are guilty, and so forth. We do not have to address these questions from the ground up every time they arise. We should try to anticipate the reactions of others, and foresee likely consequences, but while consequentialism requires us to apply a certain criterion, it does not expect us to be omniscient. Moreover, most of what we do directly affects only a small number of people, and it is not necessary to try to anticipate every "ripple in the pond" that is caused by our acts. We may be able to ascertain a great deal just by thinking care-fully about what is in people's interests or what is intrinsically good. Then, reasoning as consequentialists, we could formulate a number of secondary principles for deciding what to do and for the evaluation of actions, practices, and institutions. These may well be familiar moral rules concerning honesty, reparation for damages, promise keeping, and so forth, though they will be underwritten by consequentialist considerations.

It is also important to see that the consequentialist is not saying that we are to assess states of affairs just in terms of our own good. What morally matters is the *overall* state of the world. Suppose the theory says that happiness is the good we are to promote. There is nothing privileged about *one's own* happiness (unless one also tries to make a case for egoism). If knowledge is an intrinsic good, and one reasons as a consequentialist, then one is to promote the growth of knowledge, but not just for oneself. The case is similar for other goods. What is good is to be maximized. (The consequentialist may also argue that there is a distributional principle that should be honored, that what is good should be allocated in a certain way – but a "pure" consequentialism would make this a secondary principle, justified on the basis of how following it promotes good. Otherwise, a distributional principle such as strict equality, or making the least well off better off, or allocating benefits in accord with merit, will need its own, **non-consequentialist** justification.)

A key feature of this approach is that it does not hold that acts or action-types are right or wrong in themselves. Whether an act or practice is morally right or permissible is a matter of its consequences (or probable consequences, or intended consequences). A practice such as being honest may be generally right and we may rely on it as such, but this is not because it is intrinsically right. It is right because it is reliably good – it tends to have good consequences. There are many action-types that are characteristically good or characteristically bad, but that is not the same as being intrinsically good or bad. Indeed, there may be situations in which deliberately deceiving someone is, in consequentialist terms, the right thing to do. Or there may be situations in which limiting the liberty of even adult, rational agents may be what is morally required. The consequentialist maintains that our judgments and decisions should answer to the facts, the facts about what is best. *That* is the rational, objective way to morally judge and deliberate. If consequentialism requires some revision of our habits of moral thought, then so be it. It could very well turn out that what is consequentially justified is very much in line with what we think is intrinsically right, but we need to see that moral justification is not to be given in terms of the intrinsic rightness and wrongness of actions and practices.

Let's consider a specific issue – assisted suicide. You might think that if people who are suffering and have very dismal life prospects opt to end their lives with the assistance of a physician, then there are good reasons in favor of morally permitting them to do so. Imagine you hold this view on consequentialist grounds, not on grounds of autonomy or liberty. There very well might be consequentialist considerations in favor of respecting autonomy and extensive liberty, but in the end, they are morally supportable because of their consequences, not because of their intrinsic nature. Let us suppose you think that it is important to honor a person's wishes (assuming that the wishes were expressed at a time when the person was rational and lucid) because that is crucial to promoting the welfare of people. Further, let is suppose that needless suffering is to be minimized. On this basis, the case for assisted suicide looks quite strong.

It is easy to imagine others finding this view about the permissibility of assisted suicide morally objectionable, or even abhorrent. They might think that it is always wrong to knowingly take an innocent life, even if it is a pain-filled and miserable life, and even if it is one's own. The fact that one consents to one's life being ended, or even has a strong desire that it should be ended, does not make assisted suicide morally acceptable. There may be things that consent cannot legitimize (you might try to think of some) and this is one of them. Many people maintain that assisted suicide is *intrinsically wrong*; it is wrong even if it would prevent suffering and the person wishes to die. A consequentialist could agree that assisted suicide is wrong, but would arrive at that conclusion on different grounds. For example, it might be on the basis of concerns about abuses of its permissibility, or because it might encourage those who are ill or disabled to think of themselves as selfish burdens to others, and the like. It would be because there are reasons to think that it does not promote the best outcome; that is, it would be because of consequentialist considerations.

The non-consequentialist opponent of assisted suicide fully recognizes the badness of suffering but thinks that the wrongness of taking the sufferer's life is of primary moral significance and that its wrongness is a feature of what the action-type is in its own right. Its intrinsic features outweigh the causal difference it makes, even though suffering is awful and we may well have a duty not to increase it. The duty not to kill the innocent is, one might argue, a stronger duty than the duty not to increase or permit avoidable suffering. If you claim that the practice is intrinsically wrong, some sort of account of what makes it wrong in itself is needed. It is not good enough to just insist that it is. You need to appeal to considerations that override even an individual's considered preference and the person's consent to the means of pursuing it.

Many people have held this view about such moral matters as slavery, accusing and punishing those known to be innocent, lying, adultery, abortion, capital punishment, and suicide, among others. The good that might come of an act of these types cannot be (on this view) moral good, and it cannot morally outweigh the wrongness of the act. Consequentialists could disagree among themselves about whether assisted suicide is morally permissible. But that argument would actually be a dispute about what are the facts. They would already be agreed that the course with the best consequences is the morally right one. An argument about whether that is the correct way to interpret what is morally at stake in assisted suicide is a different argument. It is an argument between consequentialists and various types of non-consequentialist.

In addition, a consequentialist need not settle on one type or feature of states of affairs as morally significant. Mill settled on just one when he tried to explain the desirability of whatever is desirable in terms of the happiness it brought about or was part of. But a theorist might argue that value is pluralistic (of more than one type) instead of monistic (of just one type). The theory might be that knowledge is good, virtue is good, and pleasure is good but that these are independently and irreducibly good. Each is good in its own right and its goodness is not to be explained in terms of something else. Moore, for example, held that there are a number of irreducible goods. His view is a type of non-hedonistic consequentialism. The issue of whether moral value is to be interpreted monistically or pluralistically is a crucial one, but it does not on its own determine whether a theory is consequentialist or not.

Kantian Non-consequentialism

There are different versions of consequentialism, and there are also different *non-consequentialist* theories. Even though the term "non-consequentialist" is not very elegant, it marks a key distinction in the simplest way. Non-consequentialists deny that moral value is derived from or wholly located in the consequences of actions. Many non-consequentialist theories are **deontological** theories. In theories of that type the notion of rightness, or a right act is central. Such theories specify certain duties, and identify certain action-types as right or obligatory in themselves, in contrast to specifying an end or certain type of state of affairs, which is to brought about or promoted.

One of the most important non-consequentialist moral theories is Kant's. He was very deliberate and explicit about rejecting consequentialism. Kant argued that there was a distinctively moral type of obligation we are all aware of in our own experience as agents. He worked his way to the principle of duty by reflecting on the awareness of moral obligation he claimed each of us has. Even when we are strongly prompted by our desires or passions we are capable of recognizing what is morally required. Those acts are rationally necessary in an unconditional way. One acts morally when one does what is intrinsically right because it is right.

The contrast with Mill's view is striking. Mill argued that "utilitarian moralists have gone beyond almost all others in affirming that the motive has nothing to do with the morality of the action, though much to do with the worth of the agent."[6] As a consequentialist Mill was not saying that, with regard to morality, the motive morally counts for nothing. Instead, he was making a distinction between the rightness of an action and the moral worth of an agent. As he himself saw, there are certain regular connections between how one is motivated and what sorts of actions one performs. A person motivated by jealousy, spite, and narrow self-interest is not likely to perform actions that promote utility. According to Mill, though, motives are most directly relevant to evaluating agents, and we can morally assess an act without including assessment of the motive. It is the state of affairs that an act brings about (or was intended to bring about) that is the primary focus of moral evaluation.

Compare that to Kant's view: "Thus the moral worth of an action does not lie in the effect which is expected from it or in any principle of action which has to borrow its motive from this expected effect."[7] And he later writes: "The subjective ground of desire is the incentive, while the objective ground of volition is the motive. Thus arises the distinction between subjective ends, which rest on incentives, and *objective ends, which depend upon motives valid for every rational being*"[8] (emphasis added). It might have seemed to you that *of course* consideration of the consequences of acts is what should orient and structure moral thought. However, reflection might lead in a quite different direction, towards Kantian non-consequentialism. A way to pursue this issue is to notice that in your own experience you are almost certainly aware of making a distinction between the character of an action in its own right and its effects. Each of these probably seems to have moral significance, and we are sometimes perplexed about which of them has decisive moral significance. Is an action morally undermined if it was motivated by benevolence but in fact did no good or did harm? Is an action morally vindicated if it had a favorable outcome even though it was motivated by envy? It was a crucial part of Kant's view that the moral worth of an action cannot be conditioned by or contingent upon what the act brings about. As rational agents, we have control over our volitions, and we are accountable for our actions because we are the authors of our volitions. But we cannot completely control the way of the world, and it is a mistake to allow the way of the world to condition or determine the moral worth of actions.

Another crucial dimension of Kant's theory is the weight he puts on persons as ends in themselves. He wrote:

> Now, I say, man and, in general, every rational being exists as an end in himself and not merely as a means to be arbitrarily used by this or that will. In all his actions, whether they are directed to himself or to other rational beings, he must always be regarded at the very same time as an end. All objects of inclinations have only a conditional worth, for if the inclinations and the needs founded on them did not exist, their object would be without worth.[9]

Beings capable of acting according to principles they formulate themselves are owed a distinctive kind of respect and are never to be treated merely as means. They are rational agents, and as such are purposive, self-determining beings, and not just parts of the order of things governed by causal laws. They are owed respect because they can act on a law of reason, the moral law.

We are united in a common moral world by our ability to act on principles that can be endorsed by all rational agents. In so acting, we do what is rationally required and at the same time act in ways that other persons cannot find morally objectionable. There is a criterion of rightness independent of our desires and individual interests. It reflects our capacity to act on universalizable principles. In acting morally we act out of respect for principles formulated by our own rationality, rather than responding to desire and emotion or the authority of anything other than our own reason. Our nature as free, rational agents is the source and ground of moral value. Again, it is in willing in accord with moral law that we respect rational agents in the appropriate way. When our volitions have that form, they are endorsable by all rational agents.

We respect people for their talents, their accomplishments, and their efforts. We might respect or value a person for being able to put together a terrific meal in under an hour or for being an excellent athlete. But there is also a kind of respect owed to persons just on account of being persons, i.e. rational agents. They are not merely *things*. The intrinsic dignity of a person cannot be compared to the value of anything that is conditional upon desire or passion, including happiness. The respect owed to a person does not depend upon our having affection or any particular concern for that individual. It is not contingent upon how anyone *feels*. It is immune to luck. There is a reason to respect persons independent of our subjective attitudes and regard for them. We value many things because of what we desire or what our interests are, but the value of those things is conditional upon those desires and interests. The worth of persons is intrinsic and un-conditional, and that is why they are owed a distinctive kind of respect. They are ends in themselves. Acting dutifully is how we respect our-selves and other persons as autonomous, rational agents.

The moral worth of actions depends upon their being performed out of dutiful respect for moral law. Their rightness is intrinsic to them and not conditional upon what they bring about or what inter-ests they satisfy. Kant says: "There is, therefore, only one categorical imperative. It is: Act only according to that maxim by which you can at the same time will that it should become a universal law."[10] Ac-tions are morally permissible if the principles enacted can be impar-tially endorsed by all rational agents. And "to have moral worth an action must be done from duty."[11] We all have different desires, interests, emotions, and so forth. But as rational agents we are capa-ble of recognizing what is morally required independently of those conditions.

Consider the following cases. Suppose someone said to you that you ought to get a physics tutor. You are taking a physics course, and you enjoy it, and you are doing well. In that case, there is no reason for you to get a tutor, unlike the case in which you are taking a course, doing badly in it, and you want to do better in it. Then, having a physics tutor has value – but it is conditioned in just those ways. Having a physics tutor does not have value in itself. Its value is contingent upon someone's wants or needs. The value of having a certain food for dinner is conditional; it depends upon our taste or nutritional needs. The value of being Manhattan district attorney (as an end one might set oneself) is conditional; unless we had an interest in holding that office, it would not have a claim on us as something worth pursuing. There are, of course, good general reasons for why there should be a justice system and judges and other specific positions of responsibility such as district attorney. That too, however, is conditional upon certain human needs, interests, and concerns. There is nothing rationally necessary about it in its own right. The worth of persons and the way in which they are ends in themselves is not comparable to the worth of this or that end as an object of desire. The objects of desire and interest are ends that we might or might not bring about by acting. Persons, though, are "beings whose existence in itself is an end."[12]

In Kant's view, even the value of happiness is conditioned in the sense that we happen to have certain desires and it is important to us that we satisfy them, but the value of those satisfactions is contingent upon the presence of the desires. Moreover, happiness can be unmerited. A very bad person could lead a happy life if his inclinations are satisfied. That would be morally unworthy unhappiness. It would be undeserved. If the world were altogether just, then happiness would be distributed in proportion to virtue. We cannot bring about and sustain justice on that scale. What we can do, though, is make ourselves worthy of happiness by being morally good. We respect ourselves and others as ends in themselves when we act out of respect for moral law.

Like Mill, Kant sought to identify and explicate the fundamental principle of right action. The actual business of confronting specific moral matters requires consideration of the specific features of a given situation, and careful judgment that can only be cultivated by experience. That a theory maintains that there is a basic principle of right action does not imply that application of it is always easy or that there are not apparent conflicts of duty that need to be resolved. Still, Kant and Mill each held that there is a core principle of right action, a core criterion of moral worth that can be applied in a completely general way in moral judgment and reasoning. They formulated particularly explicit and clear renderings of consequentialist and non-consequentialist approaches and the reasons for them.

Intuitionist Non-consequentialism

There are important non-consequentialist moral theories that are quite different from Kant's. Some of them are *intuitionist* theories. The centerpiece of Kant's moral theory is the categorical imperative, the moral law. Intuitionist theories do not include a single fundamental principle of right action in the same way. Non-consequentialist intuitionist theories maintain that there is a plurality of moral duties of which we have immediate, uninferred knowledge. There are objective moral facts that we know intuitively, such as the fact that promises are to be kept, and that gratitude is owed to those who have helped us (if there are no countervailing or overriding considerations).

The term "intuitionism" is used in a number of senses in philosophy and we need to indicate the relevant one here. Moore, for example, noted an important distinction between senses of "intuitionism" in moral philosophy. We saw that his view was that good is an unanalyzable real object or property that we are aware of by intuition, by direct, unmediated, non-inferential awareness. Moore was an intuitionist about *how we know what is good.* However, Moore said that he was not an intuitionist in the sense that "is distinguished by maintaining that . . . propositions which assert that a certain action is right or a duty – are incapable of proof or disproof by any enquiry into the results of such actions."[13] Intuitionism in this second sense, the sense in which we have *intuitive knowledge of moral duties,* is an important type of non-consequentialism, and is the focus of our present concern. In Moore's case we have knowledge of good by intuition, but what our moral duties are is not a matter of intuitive knowledge. The intuitionism we are considering now maintains that moral requirements themselves are known intuitively.

This is not to say that it is obvious what is right and wrong or that all moral judgments are self-evident. It is the view that reflection and experience reveal that moral judgment always involves some intuitions, some uninferred knowledge of moral duties. There is no further justification for what is intuitively known. Often, we have to very carefully consider what is morally required and take into account numerous factors in judging what to do in a particular situation. For example, a situation might involve the fact that I have promised to do something, and the fact that another person needs my help, and the fact that what I am doing at present is beneficial to yet someone else. Numerous considerations are relevant and it is not at all obvious what I ought to do. But it is evident that various moral duties are involved, and I know what those are intuitively. They include, for example, the duty to keep promises and to be beneficent. The judgment of what to do and the justification of it always ultimately depend upon moral propositions or principles that we know without proof. The intuitionist argues that these are non-consequentialist duties.

Our grasp of these is not a matter of subjective conviction or feeling, it is a matter of cognition. Even if this knowledge is only attained when we are mature and experienced, we see that it is basis for specific moral judgments and not itself derived from any more basic knowledge. It may not be first in the order of time but it is first in the order of justification. W. D. Ross, a twentieth century-intutionist, wrote that when we speak of self-evidence we do not mean it:

> in the sense that it is evident from the beginning of our lives, or as soon as attend to the proposition for the first time, but in the sense that when we have reached sufficient mental maturity and have given sufficient attention to the proposition it is evident without any need of proof, or of evidence beyond itself.[14]

Bringing something into view can require careful thought even though what is brought into view does not need to be justified by being shown to *follow* from anything else. That a proposition is self-evident tells us where it stands in the order of justification. It is not a claim about obviousness. A proposition is self-evident if upon consideration of it we understand it and see that it is true − it is evident in itself and the evidence for accepting it does not come from other propositions. But there is no guarantee that self-evident truths will strike everyone who considers them as self-evident.

Ross wrote:

> We have no more direct way of access to the facts about rightness and goodness and about what things are right or good, than by thinking about them; the moral convictions of thoughtful and well-educated people are the data of ethics just as sense-perceptions are the data of a natural science.[15]

Upon reflection we find that there are numerous duties, numerous moral considerations, which properly enter our judgments about what is required. There is no further account of them any more than there is a further account (one might argue) of our basic judgments of sense perception. *They* are the starting point, the material for accounts of other judgments, and they are not reducible to judgments of one single type, based on one fundamental principle.

There are **prima facie** moral duties, such as the duties of justice, beneficence, and gratitude, which we know intuitively. That is to say, matters of justice, beneficence, and gratitude have moral significance whenever they arise. They always morally count. But in actual situations, the determination of what is our *actual* duty, our duty on the basis of the complexity of the situation and the various claims upon us, often depends upon consideration of a number of factors. Ross says of *prima facie* duties that "they are compounded together in highly complex ways."[16]

> Our judgements about our actual duty in concrete situations have none of the certainty that attaches to our recognition of the general principles of duty. A statement is certain, i.e. is an expression of knowledge, only in one or other of two cases: when it is either self-evident, or a valid conclusion from self-evident premises. And our judgements about our particular duties have neither of these characters.[17]

What is required of us in a given situation, just what is our actual duty in that case, often depends upon the presence and relations of numerous morally relevant factors. How they fit together to determine an actual duty in the instance is not self-evident.

> "*Prima facie*" suggests that one is speaking only of an appearance which a moral situation presents at first sight, and which may turn out to be illusory; whereas what I am speaking of is an objective fact involved in the nature of the situation, or more strictly in an element of its nature, though not, as duty proper does, arising from its *whole* nature.[18]

When we speak of the *whole* nature of a situation we are speaking of what we ascertain to be our *actual* duty, all things considered. Ascertaining our actual duty requires careful reflection upon *prima facie* duties and the complexities of the situation. They all count, but we have to make a judgment about which single act is right in the situation. Ross was not claiming that we have certainty about what to do, all things considered, but that we have certainty about what are *prima facie* moral duties.

Unsurprisingly, intuitionism is often criticized for failing to provide justification for moral claims and for failing to organize them in a coherent manner. John Rawls, for example, has described intuitionist theories as having two features: "first, they consist of a plurality of first principles which may conflict to give contrary directives in particular types of cases; and second, they include no explicit method, no priority rules, for weighing these principles against one another: we are simply to strike a balance by intuition, by what seems to us most nearly right."[19] The criticism that intuitionism is no more than "an unconnected heap of duties with no underlying rationale"[20] is a common one. The defender of intuitionism will argue that what might look like inadequacy of theory is actually a strength. The absence of a fundamental principle or a set of rules for deriving actual duties from general principle(s) reflects fidelity to the real complexity of moral experience. The intuitionist is responding to the fact that we are more certain of basic principles than we are of specific judgments, and that basic principles are independent of each other. Certainty of principles is one thing; certainty about just what is *the* right action, all things considered, is another.

The multiplicity of moral considerations is no argument against their objectivity, and does not render moral thought unguided or haphazard. Moral thought may not be systematic in a fixed, formal sense, but that does not mean that we cannot make clear sense of individual moral judgments and their correctness. For example, in Ross's theory there are distinctions between derived and underived duties, and between more and less general duties. These distinctions enable us to articulate what has priority and what considerations explain and justify moral judgments. Intuitionism says that justifications come to an end at a certain place – in intuitions. But that is not to say that there is no accounting for the judgments or for how they are related to each other. David McNaughton, a contemporary defender of intuitionism, observes:

> Intuitionists are skeptical about the power of abstract moral theory to answer all moral questions. They typically hold, with Aristotle, that we cannot expect more precision in ethics than the subject is capable of. It is a mistake to suppose that difficult moral issues can be definitively resolved with a high degree of certainty.[21]

Intuitionists believe there is moral knowledge but doubt that it can be codifed and organized into an overall system.

Thomas Reid, the eighteenth-century Scottish philosopher (and critic of Hume), wrote:

All reasoning must be grounded on first principles. This holds in moral reasoning, as in all other kinds. There must, therefore, be in morals, as in all other sciences, first or self-evident principles, on which all moral reasoning is grounded, and on which it ultimately rests.[22]

This is not the uncritical, complacent view that *of course* every rightly brought up person agrees that murder is wrong, that stealing is bad, and that keeping one's promises is good. It is not a point about consensus or convention but about the basis for knowledge and cognitive agreement. Intuitionists are not merely solemnizing whatever values they happen to endorse by treating them as objective constituents of reality. They are making a deeper point about how to understand the objectivity of moral judgments at the same time that we acknowledge the complexity and difficulty of many of them.

Nor need intuitionism be committed to the view that in addition to perception, memory, introspection, and reason we have an additional faculty, a special moral faculty, for detecting moral properties. Some theorists have held that we have a moral sense as a distinct faculty, but the expression "moral sense" can be used innocently to refer to the fact that we have uninferred moral knowledge, which is possible for us because we possess reason. This requires no problematic postulation of special cognitive faculties. In discussing Ross's view, McNaughton says that Ross

is not claiming that moral principles are known by some special and mysterious faculty. The only faculty involved is reason itself. Ross is here placing himself squarely in a mainstream philosophical tradition which holds that there are substantial claims whose truth we can know by direct rational insight.[23]

The ascendance of empiricism and the attendant skepticism about substantive knowledge of necessary truths by rational insight during the past century have created a philosophical atmosphere in which intuitionism has often been dismissed almost without argument. Describing a position as "intuitionism" became a quick way to disqualify it as a serious candidate. Its critics argue that it is committed to a strange metaphysics, which includes exotic value-entities, and that it requires a strange epistemology. They also have argued that we would need a faculty of intuition unlike the rest of our faculties to enable us to detect moral values or moral duties. Recall Mackie's critique of moral objectivism, which we discussed in chapter 1. It is well worth looking at the works of intuitionists to see if the charges against them are accurate and if they are as damaging as they have been widely assumed to be. It may be that there are serious problems with certain intuitionist theories that are not in fact defects of the view as such.

The Virtue-centered Approach

Consequentialism and non-consequentialism might seem to exhaust the main options. After all, the former focuses on what actions bring about, and the latter focuses on intrinsic features of acts rather than on what they bring about. But these are more like theoretical bookends than a complete range of theories. Another crucially important conception of moral considerations and moral reasoning has its source in Greek philosophy, most influentially developed by Aristotle. It differs substantially from the approaches we have discussed so far.

Mill explicitly undertook to identify what he called "the criterion of right and wrong"[24] or the "one fundamental principle or law at the root of all morality"[25] or, if there is more than one, "the rule for deciding between the various principles when they conflict".[26] Kant said of his *Foundations of the Metaphysics of Morals* that it was "nothing more than the search for and establishment of the supreme principle of morality."[27] That simply is not the project Aristotle undertook. The opening sentence of the *Nicomachean Ethics* is, "Every craft and every investigation, and likewise every action and decision, seems to aim at some good; hence the good has been well described as that at which everything aims."[28] All making, all inquiry, all action is to be understood in terms of the good that is aimed at in the undertaking. This does not itself imply that there is one single end that all undertakings aim at, but rather that human activity in general is end-oriented activity. It is intelligible with regard to the end, with regard to that-for-the-sake-of-which it is undertaken. However, this is true not just of this, that, and the other activity, but of the leading of a human life overall. Some ends are subordinate to others, and the life of a rational being is not just a sum of various activities, it is an organized, coherent arrangement of ends, concerns, and activities. Aristotle goes on to elaborate an account of overall human good, a conception of what it is best to aim at in leading one's life. This is different from formulating a principle of right action. The guiding conception can be informatively characterized, but there is no formula for leading an excellent life.

Instead of formulating a criterion of right action, Aristotle referred to the *practically wise person* as a kind of living norm, a standard of sound judgment. He wrote:

> For the excellent person judges each sort of thing correctly, and in each case what is true appears to him. For each state [of character] has its own special [view of] what is fine and pleasant, and presumably the excellent person is far superior because he sees what is true in each case, being a sort of standard and measure of what is fine and pleasant.[29]

This agent has the states of character and the capacities for judgment that enable him to recognize and appreciate the moral features of situations, and he is motivated to act in a morally sound way. As we saw in chapter 2, in the agent with Aristotelian virtue reason and desire are aligned and they pursue the same thing. As in intuitionism, the fact that morality cannot be codified or formulated in a set of rules or principles is no threat to the objectivity of moral considerations. However, one needs certain states of character to bring them clearly into view and to weigh them properly.

This is what we shall call a **virtue-centered** approach to moral theory, because the moral value of actions depends upon the extent to which they exhibit certain characteristics of the agent. This is not just a matter of what the agent brings about or intends to bring about. Nor is it just a matter of the agent's motive. It is also not just a matter of the agent's sensibility. In having the virtues an agent has a correct understanding of human good, and the agent desires to enact that understanding, and enjoys doing so. A virtue-centered approach assigns crucial and integrated roles to reason, passion, and desire.

Aristotle says that the three conditions for an agent's full-fledged possession of the virtues are: "First, he must know [that he is doing virtuous actions]; second, he must decide on them, and decide on them for themselves; and, third, he must do them from a firm and unchanging state."[30] Virtue has become second nature, and to act virtuously is a reflection of stable characteristics of the agent. When Aristotle says that the virtuous person is "a sort of standard and measure of what is fine and pleasant"[31] he does not mean that what *constitutes* acts to be fine and pleasant is that certain sorts of people (virtuous agents) perform them. It is not the fact that person P acts a certain way that makes actions of kind K right actions. The point is that the capacity to recognize what is morally required and to appreciate it in the right way depends upon the agent's habits of feeling, desire, and cognition. *That* is the sense in which the virtuous agent is a living norm. The virtuous agent is the one who is able to grasp and appreciate what is good. He has right desires, he reasons correctly, and he enjoys proper pleasures in acting. When he does an action of kind K, his performance is virtuous because of how his character is reflected in it.

By following the example of the wise and good, and by trying to understand how they see things and how they decide what to do, we will be better able to acquire the dispositions to make ourselves more wise and good. What is crucial is that we acquire genuinely virtuous habits, not just imitate the behavior of the virtuous. Coming to have the kind of understanding they have is not achieved by being presented with a collection of propositions and principles, or a theory. A person cannot be *argued* into being virtuous. The development of sound moral judgment depends upon experience and habitual practice so that the individual comes to recognize and have proper concern for the moral significance of various kinds of considerations and develops excellence at deliberating so that he can decide rightly.

The virtuous person's appreciation of situations involves correct understanding and appropriate feeling. Think, for example, of moral matters such as fairness, or courage. There are of course certain important generalizations about them. Fairness requires giving to each in accordance with their legitimate claims. Courage requires the management of fear and the exercise of judgment in facing risk and danger. We can also formulate other generalizations about why those virtues are important to our being able to lead good lives and achieve worthwhile ends. It is not as though there are no general rules about courage and fairness. But what fairness requires, or what courage requires, in a given situation depends upon the particular features of that situation and there may be few highly general principles that effectively determine judgment for actual instances. The person with the virtues has the developed abilities to make the right judgments, the abilities to see why they are right, and the motivational dispositions to perform them willingly because they are right. Both correct judgment and proper feeling are necessary if it is to be a virtuous act and not just an act that happens to be of the sort that a virtuous agent would perform.

Action-guiding moral knowledge is a highly particularized know-ledge of the features of concrete, and often quite complex, circumstances. A great deal of what practical wisdom is consists in the development of both an overall conception of a good life and fine-grained, carefully calibrated judgment about what to do in particular circumstances.

The virtuous agent who is also reflective will be able to articulate quite specific reasons for his judgments and decisions, explaining why, in a given situation, doing X was the courageous or fair thing to do. There are many things the reflective virtuous agent can say by way of explanation and justification of his or her actions, even though there may be no appeal to a completely general criterion of right action.

We should point out that neither Kant nor Mill thought that people *typically* self-consciously apply the criterion of right action by stopping and asking, "what does the Principle of Utility (or the Categorical Imperative) require me to do in this situation?" We might sometimes do that, but they recognized that we tend to act on the basis of dispositions to judge and appreciate situations in certain sorts of ways, and in that respect, they both recognized a role for the virtues. Kant and Mill both wrote about the importance of the virtues.[32] Still, in their views of morality, what makes for a virtue is the fact that the agent acts in accordance with the fundamental principle of morality (and, in Kant's view, *because* it is the fundamental principle). There is a general principle according to which right actions are right actions. In Kant's theory and Mill's theory the principle is the primary notion, and virtue is explained in terms of it. For Aristotle, virtue is basic in a way in which it is not for Kant and Mill. That is a crucial difference that is reflected in their theories overall.

The differences are explained in part by the fact that Aristotle was not answering the same kinds of questions Kant and Mill were addressing. They each had a clear sense of there being a distinctive category of practical reason concerned with "the moral" and they were identifying its special principle. But Aristotle did not distinguish the moral from the non-moral in that way. Human virtues are the states of character one needs to act well and to live well. He had a notion of human excellence that was more encompassing than Kantian or utilitarian moral excellence, and answering questions about what is a good life is different from answering questions about what are one's moral duties. Aristotle's moral theorizing is a response to a different formulation of what is most fundamentally at issue.

Like intuitionism, a virtue-centered approach denies that particular judgments are always subordinate to fixed rules. It is not clear that this is a defect. As with intuitionism, it may instead be the merit of realistically acknowledging the texture and variety of the moral dimensions of situations and actions. For example, it is plausible that honesty is not morally good in exactly the same way as generosity or fairness. Acting out of spite is not wrong in just the same way that dishonestly taking more than one's share is wrong. Cruelty is not wrong in exactly the same way as deceitful promising. The rightness of aiding those in need is not just the same as the rightness of fidelity. In each case, we can say that certain acts are right, or certain states of character are good ones to have, and certain acts are wrong, and certain states of character are bad to have. Yet in explanations of why this is so, differences will emerge between diverse goods and virtues on the one hand, and diverse evils and vices on the other. Nor is there some fixed way in which the virtues relate to each other, such that fairness always takes precedence over generosity, or beneficence over fidelity, or something like that. We need practical wisdom to make correct judgments, and that wisdom cannot be codified.

Rosalind Hursthouse, who is a defender of the virtue-centered approach, describes the objection that a virtue-centered approach lacks the formally structured resources to effectively address moral issues as follows:

> So, for example, a reviewer of fairly recent work on virtues claims that the promise that a theory of the virtues could replace deontological or utilitarian theories has not been made good and strongly implies that it cannot be. A typical critic claims that virtue ethics *cannot* answer the question "What ought I to do?" or tell us which acts are right and which wrong; and concludes that, at best, virtue ethics has a supplementary role to play, the major role to be played by an "ethics of rules."[33]

The response is that while there is no "master" principle of right action, the virtues enable us to correctly ascertain what to do and motivate us to do it. Virtues of character make us receptive and perceptive in the ways that reason understands to be correct. There is a crucial role for substantive understanding in guiding actions and for objective reasons in justifying them. The virtuous agent can see that an act was wrong *because* it was callous, ungrateful, and self-centered. Other acts are wrong for other reasons. The virtuous agent can see that an act is right *because* it is helpful, encouraging, and relieves another's anxiety. Other acts are right for other reasons. Specific concepts and categories are the concrete materials of moral life, rather than highly general ones such as right and good. An action is right or good in some specific way, and the agent with the virtues knows how to judge and choose with discernment and how to focus on details with subtlety.

Why *should* we think that there is some single moral theory that will encompass all correct moral judgments and explain them on the basis of a single criterion? Is there an *a priori* reason that tells us why moral judgments can be or must be systematized? Does experience support the conclusion that they can? What is lost, what do we do without, if they cannot be systematized?

Suppose the objector relaxes the requirement that there should be a fundamental moral law or criterion of right action. There is another serious concern about the virtue-centered approach. An oft-repeated criticism of Aristotle's view, in particular, concerns the way in which he related the virtues to human flourishing. He believed that given the constitutive capacities of human nature, there is a best kind of life for a human being, an objective conception of human good. Good action matters because of how it is constitutive of living well, of being an excellent person leading a worthwhile life. "[E]very virtue causes its possessors to be in a good state and to perform their functions well";[34] and "the virtue of a human being will likewise be the state that makes a human being good and makes him perform his function well."[35]

Even theorists who believe that there are objective goods for human beings might doubt that there is a uniquely best kind of life for a human being. It can be argued that there are many goods, and many kinds of good lives, but that there is no uniquely best conception of human perfection or successful actualization of human nature. Bernard Williams, for example, writes:

> Even if we leave the door open to a psychology that might go some way in the Aristotelian direction, it is hard to believe that an account of human nature – if it is not already an ethical theory itself – will adequately determine one kind of ethical life as against others. Aristotle saw a certain kind of ethical, cultural, and indeed political life as a harmonious culmination of human potentialities, recoverable from an absolute understanding of nature. We have no reason to believe in that.[36]

He adds that, "in its general outline the description of the ethical self we have recovered from the ancient writers is correct. At the same time, we must admit that the Aristotelian assumptions which fitted together the agent's perspective and the outside view have collapsed."[37] By the "outside view" Williams means the **teleological** conception of nature and human nature that was central to Aristotle's philosophy. That type of view of the world and our own nature has been largely abandoned, and Williams thinks that the Aristotelian account of human excellence and the virtues depended upon it. Thus while he sees great merit in Aristotle's moral philosophy, he is skeptical of whether it can be sustained in what is a very different intellectual and scientific setting.

This familiar modern doubt has motivated many thinkers to detach the notion of moral virtue from what we might call "essentialist perfectionism." That is the view: (a) that there is a proper end for a human being; (b) that it depends upon the distinctive capacities of human nature; and (c) that the virtues are the excellences that enable a person to engage in the activities that realize that end. A theorist might maintain that the virtues are fundamental to the account of morality without also interpreting them with reference to a single, objective end for a human life overall, determined by human nature. Perhaps there are certain states of character that are needed in order for human beings to live well, but they are not to be interpreted with regard to a specific notion of human flourishing. (This connection between the virtues and leading a good life is one way in which virtue-centered theorizing differs from many versions of intuitionism.)

Historically, the connection between the virtues and a conception of human flourishing has been very important. You might consider whether it is possible to present a virtue-centered account of moral judgment and good action without presenting it as part of a larger conception of what is the best kind of life. We will not pursue the question here, but only point to it as an important issue for reflection and analysis. It is an important question and one that is related to other differences between, say, Aristotle on the one hand, and Kant and Mill on the other. Often conceptions of the virtues are parts of overall conceptions of human good, rather than being tied to a distinctly moral sphere of practical reasoning. In that respect, disputes between virtue theorists and other theorists involve basic issues about what is being looked for in moral theorizing and the way in which morality figures in a life overall. The discussion of different interpretations of naturalism in chapter 4 will help explain *why* Aristotle developed the kind of theory he did. That is not our present focus of concern, and at this juncture we will take a look at another important general approach to moral theorizing.

Contractarianism

The notion of a social contract has been prominent in the modern tradition of moral theorizing, stretching back to the seventeenth century. The central idea of the **contractarian** approach is that morality is based on principles that people have reason to accept upon careful consideration of their interests and consideration of the difference it would make to them to be participants in a cooperative social scheme in which those principles are upheld. The main issue is what an agent has good reason to endorse as binding, as establishing obligations. You might think that, in a general sense, this is true of just about any approach to moral theory. After all, the utilitarian could argue that there are reasons for agents to endorse utilitarianism, because the utilitarian claims have to have a true conception of the good. The virtue theorist could argue that there are reasons for people to endorse that view, because that theorist claims to have a true conception of what states of character are needed in order for people to judge and act well. The intuitionist might say that moral intuitions, when correctly understood, merit or demand our rational assent. However, the contract theorist constructs moral theory in such a way that the notion of rational agreement is basic. Moral requirements have a claim upon us *because* of our rational acceptance or endorsement of them. In general, contract theorists argue that there are no moral facts or true moral principles independent of what is agreed to by a procedure of rational acceptance.

Such theories tend to put special weight on the social dimension of morality. Part of what is involved in the notion of rational agreement is the issue of *why* an agent would comply with rules and principles governing conduct, and this issue concerns relations between agents in a social order. Even egoists share a social world. Thus, contract theories tend to focus on basic principles of justice and what fundamental arrangements are necessary for a well ordered civil society.

In the early modern period, the contract approach was a way of detaching moral authority and political legitimacy from various religious, cultural, and historical traditions and a way of requiring that their rationale be much more transparent. In the classic contract theories of Thomas Hobbes and John Locke the notion of the state of nature is employed (differently by each theorist) to articulate a conception of pre-civil human nature and the human condition. In that condition there are no authorized institutional arrangements through which violations of rights and other wrongs are addressed and redressed. There is no rationally agreed upon normative order or recognized civic authority. Each person's life and property are as precarious as everyone else's. The state that results from the contract is structured in accord with principles that all have accepted for similar reasons.

Part of Hobbes's greatness is his role in conceptualizing political institutions as artifacts constructed by human rationality. This was a crucial development because it put political theory on a foundation of rational choice. Hobbes himself defended a theory in which the rule of the sovereign determined law and justice. Still, his view that entering into the social contract was a step taken by a rational agent to protect and promote his own interests has proved to be an important basis for a great deal of modern liberal political thought. The state's legitimacy is grounded in the rational consent of those who are members of it. For his part, Locke's theorizing has been enormously important to modern political theory because of the way it explains limitations on state power and the way it justifies basic rights, including private property. It has been one of the main influences on the modern liberal tradition and the understanding of natural rights, individual liberty, limitations on state power, and the legitimacy of political authority.

In an influential recent version of contract theorizing John Rawls says:

> the guiding idea is that the principles of justice for the basic structure of society are the object of the original agreement. They are the principles that free and rational persons concerned to further their own interests would accept in an initial position of equality as defining the fundamental terms of their association.[38]

Rawls maintains that on the contract doctrine, "we think of a well-ordered society as a scheme of cooperation for reciprocal advantage regulated by principles which persons would choose in an initial situation that is fair,"[39] and that "On a contract doctrine the moral facts are determined by the principles which would be chosen in the original position."[40] In the **original position** you do not know what your position will be in the actual circumstances, and that should prevent you from selecting principles just because they will help you preserve advantages you presently have. You simply have to proceed as a rational agent concerned with your own interests, but you do not know how well off you are naturally and socially. You do not know what will be your actual position in society once the "veil of ignorance" of the original position is lifted. The "veil of ignorance" ensures that "no one knows his place in society, his class position or social status, nor does any one know his fortune in the distribution of natural assets and abilities, his intelligence, strength, and the like."[41] That ignorance should keep your endorsements from reflecting bias.

There are, though, many things about the world in general that one does know in the original position, according to Rawls's theory. Each agent is supposed to have general knowledge of psychology, sociology, and economics. Still, in the original position the "veil of ignorance" guarantees that no one "is able to design principles to favor his particular condition,"[42] and so, "the principles of justice are the result of a fair agreement or bargain."[43] Rawls argues that this is a strategy for arriving at basic principles of justice and basic social arrangements that merit the allegiance of all rational agents. The "original position" and the "veil of ignorance" are hypothetical devices for constructing those principles and the arrangements that secure their realization in a social world. According to the contract theorist, we ascertain correct moral principles not by a metaphysical investigation of value or by reading value off of facts about human nature, but by determining which stable agreements people see as reasonable, with each arriving at their conclusion from a standpoint of equality.

Rawls acknowledges a considerable debt to Kant and this can be seen in the way his view "joins the content of justice with a certain conception of the person; and this conception regards persons as both free and equal."[44] He says, "Kantian constructivism holds that moral objectivity is to be understood in terms of a suitably constructed social point of view that all can accept."[45] He does not take over Kant's metaphysical conception of rational agency and pure practical reason but he sees the project of rational contract as shaped by a conception of the autonomous agent – a notion of fundamental importance to

Kant's theorizing. For reasons having to do with his Kantian commitments Rawls's results are non-utilitarian. He believes that utilitarianism fails to adequately recognize and respect persons as "free and equal" because of its overriding concern with promoting the best overall state of affairs.

The theoretical devices employed by Rawls are not necessarily components of the contract approach, and other contract theorists describe the initial circumstances of the participants and their procedures quite differently. While the notion of rational agreement is the centerpiece of contract theory, different versions of it are diverse in their starting points, strategies, and results. Much of the work is done in describing the parties to the contract – in presenting a conception of the rational agent and his basic interests and concerns. Those will powerfully influence the conception of what it is rational to agree to and comply with. For example, David Gauthier argues that the appropriate conditions for fashioning the contract are satisfied:

> not by placing the bargainers behind a veil of ignorance, but rather by taking each to be adequately informed not only about his own good but also about that of his fellows. Communication among the persons must be full and free; no one is able to deceive another about anyone's interests or bluff successfully about what anyone is willing to do.[46]

He says that "we require that the process of bargaining exhibit procedural equality and maximum competence among the persons who are to agree on the principles of justice."[47] In this way, parties to the contract are best able to ensure that the result is a fair cooperative arrangement that promotes mutual benefit. In Gauthier's approach there is no veil of ignorance, and communication between agents is crucial to determining the terms of the contract. Rawls described the conditions of contract in a way that eliminated bargaining between parties to it, while Gauthier deliberately builds in bargaining as part of the strategy of fashioning a just agreement.

Thomas Scanlon conceives the circumstances of contract differently. His main concern is what it would be reasonable to agree to and unreasonable to reject on the basis of justificatory considerations agents offer each other, assuming they share the desire to agree on principles they could not reasonably reject. Scanlon proceeds by putting special weight on what "no one could reasonably reject as a basis for informed, unforced general agreement."[48] This is because:

[the] only relevant pressure for agreement comes from the desire to find and agree on principles which no one who had this desire could reasonably reject. According to contractualism, moral argument concerns the possibility of agreement among persons who are all moved by this desire, And moved by it to the same degree.[49]

He adds that, "contractualism [in contrast to, say, utilitarianism] seeks to explain the justificatory status of moral properties, as well as their motivational force, in terms of the notion of reasonable agreement."[50] This is a different strategy of construction for the contract, with a different description of the normative aspirations of the parties to the contract.

As we noted above, a theorist's interpretation of the starting position of the contracting parties will shape the account of what principles they can mutually and rationally agree on. In order to give this account in an illuminating way, the contract theorist needs to supply a picture of what a rational agent is like, and also what situation the agent is in as a potential party to the contract. The theorist needs some controlling interpretation of what sorts of considerations are crucial to a rational agent considering what to agree to and how that agent weighs those considerations. Are agents basically egoists? Are they concerned with mutual benefit or only their own predicaments? Are they naturally disposed to seek the welfare of others? What sorts of rights and liberties are of most fundamental concern to them? Is commitment to morality or fear of punishment the main motive for compliance? And so forth.

Moreover, what it is like in the postulated pre-civil condition can be important to ascertaining the main principles of a social world that is meant to be stable, morally ordered, and worth participating in. The differences between Hobbes's and Locke's interpretations of the pre-civil condition of agents in the state of nature provide an excellent illustration of this point. The conception of pre-contract agents and their circumstances is crucial in the work of more recent contract theorists as well. The contract theorist also needs to supply an account of the procedure of contract – something that we have seen can be conceived in quite different ways. Just what is the method of arriving at a rational agreement? In these respects the initial commitments of the theory are important indicators of where the theory is headed, and the starting points are often the most disputed parts of the theory.

The contractarian approach to moral theory is open to different sorts of results. The results may be utilitarian principles, principles of overall mutual advantage, principles of equality, *maximin* principles (according to which the minimum level of welfare of parties to the contract is to be maximized), or other principles. The specific content of moral theory that is arrived at depends upon the theorist's view of the nature of rational agents and what is most in their interest. Is it personal autonomy and political liberty, or improving their conditions and prospects, or minimizing the risk of being and remaining badly off, or reducing the inequalities that inevitably emerge?

The contractarian approach is designed to filter out various kinds of differences in people's situations, outlooks, preferences, and abilities, and to overcome the influence of bias, ideology, and complacency. Still, the demands of morality that people will agree to depend upon their antecedent conceptions of their interests, moral ideals, knowledge, and so forth. Some of this may be modified by the (hypothetical) debate that precedes the contract, but people come to the debate with certain substantive conceptions even if they are willing to critically discuss these in good faith and go through a dialectical process of challenge, refinement, and reconsideration. Within the contractarian approach to moral theory much of the debate concerns how to interpret the rationality of agents who are parties to the contract, and how to specify just what is at stake in fashioning an agreement all would enter into.

Theories, Duties, and Metaethics

We have looked at conceptions of the source and "location" of moral value and how those conceptions shape moral theories. There are quite different answers to the question "what should we look to in order to ascertain the moral worth of an action or situation?" or "what is the basis of moral principles?" Different answers to these questions yield different accounts of the architecture of moral theory and moral reasoning.

Some of the differences are quite sharp. However, despite the differences any moral theory will be a theory about what we ought to do. For example, the concept of duty is explicitly at the center of Kant's theory. While Mill did not believe that duty is a motive necessary for right action, he held that the application of the principle of utility enables us to ascertain what are our duties. Aristotle held that the virtues enable us to know what is required and also motivate us to do it. As we have noted, he did not carve out a distinctively moral sphere of practical rationality, but the agent with the virtues acts in the ways that he does because he recognizes certain actions as what he must do, as practically necessary. Contract theorists argue that real or hypothetical agreements yield practical requirements of a distinctively moral character to which we owe compliance. A divine command theory of morality is obviously a theory of what are people's duties. (We will discuss theistically based morality in chapter 4.) All of these approaches are attempts to answer basic questions about what sorts of requirements should concern us as not merely discretionary.

The various positions largely share the idiom of "obligation," "duty," "morally required," and the like. They are divided by their different interpretations of how to explain that idiom. Disputes about the nature of value and the ground of moral requirements can go on while all the parties to the disputes agree that moral considerations have a special importance. If a person has borrowed some money and made a promise to repay it, then he has an obligation to repay it. He cannot wriggle out of the obligation by giving a metaethical argument that there are no objective values. Or imagine someone saying, "Yes, I know I promised, but I did not contractually commit myself to keeping promises." Apart from the moral nihilist (the person who thinks that moral requirements are illusory or counterfeit), all the parties to these controversies agree that they are trying to account for the way in which requirements are to be understood. This is not exactly the same issue as the normative question of what precisely *are* our moral obligations. That is an argument about the content of moral theory rather than its form.

The approaches to moral theory we have discussed are not the only ones but they give us a good idea of the considerations that motivate different approaches and also some of the crucial distinctions between them. It is not essential that a moral theory be strictly of just one type, though it is important that it should have a coherent overall structure. Purity is not the main concern. Of course, we cannot just use whatever conceptual resources are needed to get things to "come out" the way we want them to. That would be intellectually irresponsible. Rather, making the best sense of moral reasoning and giving the best guidance to it is what matters most. In being responsive to our best understanding of the weight and character of different moral considerations we may find that our theory cannot be fully elaborated along the lines of just one type of approach. It may involve acknowledging more than one source or locus of moral value.

A good example of a theorist wrestling with the issue of how to give overall coherence to seemingly disparate moral considerations is Mill. In chapters 4 and 5 of *Utilitarianism* he tries to show how virtue (chapter 4) and justice (chapter 5) can be explained on utilitarian grounds. He was anxious to show that, ultimately, utility alone is the determinant of moral value. Yet virtue and justice certainly *seem* to many people to have a claim on us as moral matters independent of considerations of utility. Virtues, excellences of character, seem to have value in their own right, independent of utility. It may be that virtuous activity makes for a happier life, but virtue is not morally commendable only because it contributes to or is part of happiness. Similarly, considerations of justice seem to have a standing independent of utility and, indeed, seem to be quite different from it. You should be able to think of cases in which utility and justice seem to pull in different directions. If all this is true, then perhaps utility cannot be the sole, fundamental value and there are other (non-consequentialist) sources of value.

Mill confronts this challenge head on and tries to defeat it. You might examine his arguments carefully to see how well he succeeds in the attempt. In doing so, look at the ways in which Mill's claims about moral psychology – in particular his claims about the role of the sentiments and about the desire for happiness – figure in his attempts to "domesticate" virtue and justice to utility. They are very important to the overall case for utilitarianism and its monistic theory of value and consequentialist structure.

You might also consider the ways in which a Kantian would address situations in which acting on the categorical imperative is complicated by what seem to be conflicts of duties. Are there genuine conflicts of duties and, if so, how does a theory that bases duties on a single principle resolve them? Also, can we conceive of circumstances in which acting on the categorical imperative would have disastrous consequences, and should that motivate a reconsideration of its uniqueness as the criterion of right action?

When we are actually deliberating (rather than theorizing) we probably do not explicitly employ the terms of one or another of these theories, but we *are* thinking in ways that are described and explained by them. Most of us have habits of judgment and reasoning that have become largely second nature and we employ them without theoretically articulating them. The import of a moral theory is that it gives a systematic, rigorous articulation of the character and elements of moral thought. That is not only philosophically illuminating. It can also make a difference to what we decide and what we do. A clearer conception of presuppositions, implications, and justificatory considerations can help us critically reflect on our own views and judgments, and may lead us to refine or revise them. At the very least, it shows that moral thought is not a mere assemblage of convictions and commitments but can and should have a general, coherent character.

Where Now?

We have examined fundamental questions about the status of moral value, some of the main topics of moral psychology, and the structure of moral theory. In chapter 4 we will examine different views of the relation between moral value and non-moral facts and properties. For example, if a person attacks another without provocation and enjoys hurting his victim, we say that the action was cruel and also wrong. How is the moral feature of the act related to its other features? How is the *wrongness* of cruelty related to facts about what cruelty is? Is it simply a matter of definition or is there some more substantive relation between them? Similarly, how is the justice (or injustice) of a practice or a situation related to facts about that practice or that situation?

Even if moral value is objective, we need to specify the character of that objectivity and the way in which moral value is or is not related to non-moral features of the world. Many theorists argue that there are objective facts about the natural world and the social world, but moral values are not parts or constituents of those. They hold that moral judgments are expressions of our feelings, or they reflect commitments or stances we have adopted. Still, even in that case it seems there could be important relations between facts about the natural and social worlds on the one hand, and morality on the other. We say that this or that action is morally good or morally bad *because* it is an act of a certain type – because it has certain non-moral properties. Not just any action can be (plausibly) regarded as wrong, for example. We now turn to various conceptions of the relation between moral value and non-moral facts, and what philosophically motivates those conceptions.

Questions for Discussion and Reflection

1　Contrast the way in which Mill understands virtue and the way in which Aristotle understands it. How successful is Mill's attempt to show that virtue and its importance can be explained in utilitarian terms?

2　Discuss the different ways in which egoism might be a concern for different basic approaches to moral theorizing. Is there an egoist challenge that successful moral theorizing must defeat or deflate?

3　Kant's theory has a role for virtue, but why would Kant find a virtue-centered moral theory (e.g. Aristotle's theory) to be fundamentally flawed and inadequate as a theory of morality?

4　What might be some main points of contention between contractarians and intuitionists? They could find themselves agreeing on many moral matters; but what are the main differences in their approaches to justification?

5　In what ways (if any) would it be necessary for the most adequate moral theory to include both consequentialist and non-consequentialist considerations?

6　In reflecting on your own moral convictions and beliefs, does it seem that one or another basic strategy of moral theorizing best captures and expresses their basic features? Does it seem to you that there *is* a coherent overall pattern to the way in which you think about moral matters?

Thinkers and Their Works, and Further Reading

Aristotle: *Nicomachean Ethics*
David Gauthier: "Justice as Social Choice"; *Morals By Agreement*
Rosalind Hursthouse: "Applying Virtue Ethics"
Immanuel Kant: *Foundations of the Metaphysics of Morals*
John Locke: *Second Treatise of Government*
David McNaughton: "Intuitionism"; *Moral Vision*
J. S. Mill: *Utilitarianism*
G. E. Moore: *Principia Ethica*
John Rawls: *A Theory of Justice*; "Kantian Constructivism in Moral Theory"

Thomas Reid: *Essays on the Active Powers*

W. D. Ross: *The Right and the Good*

Thomas Scanlon: "Contractualism and Utilitarianism"; *What We Owe to Each Other*

Bernard Williams: *Ethics and the Limits of Philosophy*; *Utilitarianism: For and Against* (co-written with J. J. C. Smart)

Notes

1   A distinction is often drawn between act-utilitarianism and rule-utilitarianism. The former is the view that individual acts are to be assessed in determining what is morally required. The latter is the view that it is the utility of following general rules or principles that is to be considered in making judgments of utility. A rule can be justified by its utility and it may be best to adhere to the rule (because of its utility) even if in individual cases there would occasionally be more utility in violating the rule. An act is right if it is in accord with a justified rule, on this view. The act-utilitarian insists that each act is to be judged on its own utilitarian merits. Mill's own work is not entirely clear with regard to whether he is an act-utilitarian or rule-utilitarian.

2   J. S. Mill, *Utilitarianism* (Indianapolis: Hackett Publishing Company, 1979), p. 3.

3   Ibid., pp. 37–8.

4   Ibid., p. 7.

5   Ibid., p. 21.

6   Ibid., p. 18.

7   Immanuel Kant, *Foundations of the Metaphysics of Morals*, trans. Lewis White Beck (Indianapolis: Bobbs-Merrill, 1976), p. 17.

8   Ibid., p. 45.

9   Ibid., p. 46.

10   Ibid., p. 39.

11   Ibid., p. 16.

12   Ibid., p. 46.

13   G. E. Moore, *Principia Ethica* (Cambridge: Cambridge University Press, 1994), p. 35.

14   W. D. Ross, *The Right and The Good* (Oxford: Clarendon Press, 1930), p. 29.

15   Ibid., pp. 40–1.

16   Ibid., p. 27.

17   Ibid., p. 30.

18   Ibid., p. 20.

19   John Rawls, *A Theory of Justice* (Cambridge, MA: Harvard University Press, 1971), p. 34.

20   Ibid., p. 27.

21   David McNaughton, "Intuitionism," in *The Blackwell Guide to Ethical Theory*, ed. Hugh LaFollette (Oxford: Blackwell Publishers, 2000), p. 271. Aristotle, commenting on the way in which moral claims should not be expected to fit into a rigid system, remarks: "the educated person seeks exactness in each area to the extent that the nature of the subject allows; for apparently it is just as mistaken to demand demonstrations from a rhetorician as to accept [merely] persuasive arguments from a mathematician" (*Nicomachean Ethics*, 1094b, 24–6). In addition, the intelligence that makes for excellent moral judgment "is concerned with particulars as well as universals, and particulars become known from experience" (ibid., 1142a, 15).

22   Thomas Reid, *Essays on the Active Powers*, excerpted in *Inquiry and Essays*, ed. Ronald E. Beanblossom and Keith Lehrer (Indianapolis: Hackett Publishing Company, 1983), p. 321.

23   McNaughton, "Intuitionism," p. 282.

24   Mill, *Utilitarianism*, p. 1.

25   Ibid., p. 3.

26   Ibid., p. 3.

27   Kant, *Foundations of the Metaphysics of Morals*, p. 8.

28   Aristotle, *Nicomachean Ethics*, trans. Terence Irwin (Indianapolis: Hackett Publishing Company, Inc., 1985), 1094a, 1–3.

29   Ibid., 1113b, 33.

30   Ibid., 1105a, 30–2.

31   Ibid., 1113a, 33–4.

32   See chapter four of J. S. Mill's *Utilitarianism* and Kant's *Doctrine of Virtue* for discussions of the nature and role of virtue.

33   Rosalind Hursthouse, "Applying Virtue Ethics," in *Virtues and Reasons*, ed. Rosalind Hursthouse, Gavin Lawrence, and Warren Quinn (Oxford: Clarendon Press, 1998), p. 58.

34   Aristotle, *Nicomachean Ethics*, 1106a, 16.

35   Ibid., 1106a, 23–4.

36   Bernard Williams, *Ethics and the Limits of Philosophy* (Cambridge: Harvard University Press, 1985), p. 52.

37   Ibid., pp. 52–3.

38   Rawls, *A Theory of Justice*, p. 11.

39   Ibid., p. 33.

40   Ibid., p. 45.

41   Ibid., p. 12.

42   Ibid.

43   Ibid.

44 John Rawls, "Kantian Constructivism in Moral Theory," in *Moral Discourse and Practice*, ed. Stephen Darwall, Allan Gibbard, and Peter Railton (New York: Oxford University Press, 1997), p. 248.

45 Ibid.

46 David Gauthier, "Justice as Social Choice," in *Morality, Reason and Truth*, ed. David Copp and David Zimmerman (Totowa, NJ: Rowman and Allanheld, 1985), p. 257.

47 Ibid.

48 Thomas Scanlon, "Contractualism and Utilitarianism," in *Moral Discourse and Practice*, ed. Stephen Darwall, Allan Gibbard, and Peter Railton (New York: Oxford University Press, 1997), p. 272.

49 Ibid., p. 273.

50 Ibid., p. 277.

4 Naturalism and Non-naturalism

We have looked at a range of positions on the issue of objectivity and subjectivity, at central issues of moral psychology, at conceptions of the source or locus of moral value, and at how all of these bear on the structure of moral theories and the character of moral reasoning. One further matter needs to be taken up. It concerns the relation between moral value and non-moral considerations, and, in particular, natural facts and properties. This is an important metaethical issue in its own right and also an excellent way to connect the topics of this book with philosophy more widely. After all, exploring the relation between moral values and non-moral facts and properties is like asking, "Where (if anywhere) in the world is moral value?" In answering that question we are examining conceptions of what sorts of things there are in the world, how they are related, and how we can have knowledge of them.

One very basic division between views on this matter concerns whether moral value should be interpreted naturalistically. We will look at views from both sides of that divide. In addition, we will see that there are several different conceptions of naturalism. In chapter 1 we saw that the interpretation of objectivity is philosophically contested, and we will find that the same is true of naturalism. We will start with a highly general characterization of it, and as the chapter proceeds we will examine diverse interpretations of it and the reasons for embracing naturalism and for rejecting it.

Naturalism

Naturalism is a view about what there is. While there is no single interpretation of naturalism that all agree is correct, it clearly contrasts with supernaturalism. The naturalist holds that the whole of reality includes nothing beyond or outside of nature (and the things that natural beings make, such as candles, shoes, communications satellites, automobiles, and sofa-beds). This leaves open exactly how nature is to be understood, but it is still an important claim. It is often joined with the claim that the sciences, if they were complete and accurate, would tell us all there is to say about what there is and what it is like, because there is nothing supernatural or transcendent. Human beings are natural beings, the world does not contain any super- or **non-natural** beings, and the methods of inquiry that humans are able to develop are adequate for explaining natural phenomena.

Naturalism is also an important position concerning the justification of knowledge claims. In particular, it contrasts with rationalism, which holds that reason or the intellect, independent of the senses, is a (or *the*) faculty of knowledge and that genuine knowledge is rational knowledge (as opposed to beliefs acquired by sense perception and methods of empirical inquiry). Naturalism rejects metaphysics and *a priori* theorizing as strategies for achieving knowledge. The epistemological naturalist argues that justified belief is to be explained in terms of causal processes of belief-formation and belief-acceptance rather than in terms of *a priori* norms. Naturalists argue that reason itself is a natural capacity and its character and operation can be understood through the methods of the sciences instead of according to purely *a priori* methods. At the most general level, it is safe to say that naturalism is a rejection of rationalist metaphysics and epistemology. This is why the contrasts between Descartes and Hume are excellent resources for exploring naturalism. The same is true of the contrasts between Plato and Hume.

The progress of the sciences has given considerable impetus to naturalism in moral theorizing and in other areas of philosophy (e.g. philosophy of mind, metaphysics, epistemology). It has led many philosophers to think that perhaps a fully naturalistic conception of the world can be adequate and true. We can explain what there is, and how it works (including the creatures like ourselves who think and inquire), in terms of the natural (and social) sciences without any commitment to supernatural or non-natural entities, agencies, or processes. It is, however, possible to endorse naturalism in one area without endorsing global naturalism, naturalism about everything. One might take the view that whatever else reality might comprise, there is nothing metaphysically distinct about moral value in particular, and a complete account of it can be given in naturalistic terms. Maybe you do not have a view about the whole of reality but you believe there are decisive reasons to interpret moral value naturalistically. This way, moral value would be demystified; it would be fitted into our overall conception of nature. Some naturalists aspire to fit moral values into a scientific conception of the world and want to show that they can be quite clearly and exhaustively understood in terms of the sorts of entities and properties that scientific theories refer to. Other naturalists are less anxious to treat moral properties in a scientific manner and are mainly concerned to show that moral values can be interpreted without commitment to anything outside of the natural order.

There is a lively, ongoing debate about the proper interpretation of naturalism, but it is plain that if Plato's form of the good exists, then moral value is not naturalistic. Kant's account of moral value in terms of pure practical reason is a non-natural account. Moore's good is non-natural. According to theistic views, God exists and is the source and ground of true morality, and for that reason, moral value is not naturalistic. In our discussions in the preceding chapters we have encountered naturalistic views and non-naturalistic ones. Whatever one's account of moral value, it will involve taking a stand on the question of naturalism, either explicitly or implicitly, and the reasons for taking that stand will be of the first importance.

Before we go into the details of any specific views it will be helpful to identify some of the main possibilities for the relation between moral value and non-moral facts and properties. These are different answers to the question of how moral values are related to the rest of what there is.

1   Moral values can be *defined or analyzed* in terms of natural facts and properties.
2   Moral values are *constituted* by natural properties.
3   Moral values are not identical with, but are *dependent* upon certain natural properties.
4   Moral values are identical with certain natural facts and properties, but cannot be defined in terms of them. (The relation between

the moral and the non-moral cannot be specified in terms of identity of meaning.)

5   Moral values have a *fully independent* standing and nature, and are neither dependent upon, nor definable in terms of, natural facts and properties.

6   Moral values are not constituents of the natural world, nor are they non-natural entities or properties. Rather, moral claims are *to be understood expressively*. When we make moral judgments we express attitudes, responses, or stances, but report no facts. Moral terms are meaningful but not by virtue of referring to objects. Their meaning is expressive.

7   Moral values have a supernatural origin and ground in God.

These are not all of the possibilities, but they do give us a good sense of the overall landscape of the issue. You should be able to see that there are important connections between these views and the views about the status of moral values, the issue of cognitivism, and the possibility of moral knowledge that we looked at in chapter 1. If (1), (2), or (4) is true, then if we have knowledge of the relevant naturalistic considerations, we can also have at least some moral knowledge. In those views, the methods of acquiring moral knowledge are not fundamentally distinct from the methods for acquiring non-moral empirical knowledge. Of course, we need to employ moral *concepts* (such as wrong, right, unfair, virtuous, obligatory) in order to have moral knowledge. Yet those concepts would not refer to anything outside of the natural order. On the views in question there is, for example, no *a priori* Kantian project of analyzing the structure of pure practical reason to ascertain the nature of moral value. Similarly, there is no Platonic project of seeking a comprehension of good that is an object of the intellect in a supersensible order.

If (5) is true, the situation is quite different. Naturalism could not be a totally adequate account of what there is and the theorist defending (5) would also need to give an account of how we encounter values, how we know them. Plato held a view that falls in the category picked out by (5), and so did Kant. According to Plato, good is a non-natural, supersensible reality. According to Kant, what makes the good will good is volition that is structured by the categorical imperative; it wills what is right because it is right. This kind of volition is not, according to Kant, an event or activity in the natural or empirical order, and the law of the good will is not a law of nature. It is a rational, moral law.

If (3) is true, there is room for a number of different possibilities, shaped by how the dependence is specified. An account of type (3) could be a naturalistic account, but it could also be a version of non-naturalism. According to (6), there is no objective moral value, and value is to be understood in terms of human subjectivity. When we make moral judgments we are expressing stances or attitudes, not reporting what is morally the case. When we examine this view we will see that though it denies that there are naturalistic moral values, it holds that morality involves nothing non-natural. Moral language is not to be interpreted in terms of referring to moral properties or moral facts of any kind. This will be clarified below. We will also discuss (7) and the way in which theism has been held to be crucial to a full account of moral value and moral obligation.

The Modern Debate about Naturalism

We shall enter the issues by looking at some of G. E. Moore's main claims and arguments. His work is an especially apt starting point because much of the debate since his time has been motivated by his views and the responses to them. The issues predate Moore but he pushed the debate about naturalism onto centerstage in an explicit way. (His most influential work, *Principia Ethica*, was first published in 1903.)

Moore famously argued that *any* attempt to define good – whether in naturalistic or non-naturalistic terms, is fallacious. He said: "If I am asked 'What is good?' my answer is that good is good, and that is the end of the matter. Or if I am asked 'How is good to be defined?' my answer is that it cannot be defined, and that is all I have to say about it."[1] Any attempt to define fundamental moral terms in non-moral terms must fail, because the moral is distinct from the non-moral and cannot be reduced to it or analyzed into it. There are moral facts; for example, if X is good it is a moral fact that it is. But moral facts are distinctively *moral* facts, and cannot be defined in terms of any other kind. Moore wrote:

> It may be true that all things which are good are *also* something else, just as it is true that all things which are yellow produce a certain kind of vibration in the light. And it is a fact, that Ethics aims at discovering what are those other properties belonging to all things which are good.

But far too many philosophers have thought that when they named those other properties they were actually defining good; that these properties, in fact, were simply not "other," but absolutely and entirely the same with goodness. This view I propose to call the "naturalistic fallacy" and of it I shall now endeavor to dispose.[2]

We should note that Moore was interested in *real* definition and not verbal definition. He said that he wanted to know what good is, not what is the "proper usage, as established by custom"[3] of the word "good." A verbal definition would tell us what is a linguistic equivalent or substitute for "good," or what is the rule for its use. A real definition would tell us *what good is*.

Moore's denial that there is any real definition of good might sound like a refusal to even take the issue seriously. After all, we can say of anything that it is what it is and that it is not another thing. That is true, but not very illuminating. But Moore was not being merely stubborn, or evading the issue of how good is to be defined. He claimed to be presenting decisive arguments that good cannot be defined and, though it cannot be defined, that casts no doubt on the reality of good or our knowledge of it. He insisted that when we make a moral judgment we are using at least one moral concept that is irreducible to non-moral terms. There just is no analysis of it in other terms. (Maybe *right* can be defined in terms of *good*, e.g. an act is right if it maximizes the good. But there will be at least one moral concept that cannot be defined, and Moore thought that was *good*.) He called the attempt to define good the "naturalistic fallacy," arguing that whether it is defined in naturalistic terms or any others, the attempt must fail. Good is real, objective, and indefinable.

Moore also argued that it is "always an open question whether anything that is natural is good."[4] The strategy of the open-question argument has proved to be extremely influential and is still of great importance in theorizing about morality. Suppose someone *defines* good as happiness. It may be that happiness is indeed a good thing. Still, Moore insists that it is a genuine question, the answer to which we must find out, whether good is just the same thing as happiness. If it were a matter of definition – if "good" just meant "happiness" because they are definitionally equivalent, there would be no open question. The matter would be settled by what the words mean. Someone who denied the synonymy would exhibit a lack of fluency with the term "good." Tigers are carnivorous, but "tiger" and "carnivorous" do not mean exactly the same. The question whether tigers are carnivorous is a genuine question. Moore's concern was that if intrinsic value (good) were analyzable into any non-moral terms, then good would be wholly assimilated to something non-moral. But good is what *it* is, and not any other thing.

Suppose we define good as D. (You can fill in D with different content, according to what you take good to be.) If "D" is "pleasant and desirable" and we ask "Is what is pleasant and desirable, pleasant and desirable?" we are not asking an open question. If we ask "Is what is pleasant and desirable also good?" we are asking an open question. Again, it may be that things that are D are good things, but that does not show that good and D are identical or that "good" and "D" have exactly the same meaning.

In chapter 1 we noted that hedonistic utilitarianism interprets moral value in terms of what it claims is the only thing desirable for its own sake, and only for its own sake, namely pleasure. Other things are desirable, but they are desirable for the sake of it. For that reason, Mill, for example, argued that it is good. Is this an account of the sort Moore was criticizing? If it is a straightforward definitional claim about "good," then it would seem to fall victim to what Moore called the "naturalistic fallacy."

Moore certainly *thought* Mill was attempting to define moral value in non-moral terms. What Mill actually said is this: "The utilitarian doctrine is that happiness is desirable, and the only thing desirable, as an end; all other things being desirable as means to that end."[5] And "to think of an object as desirable (unless for the sake of its consequences) and to think of it as pleasant are one and the same thing; and that to desire anything except in proportion as the idea of it is pleasant is a physical and metaphysical impossibility."[6] He does not actually come right out and say that he is *defining* good in terms of pleasure or what is desirable, but we can see how he might be interpreted as indicating that that is how good is to be understood. You might look at Mill's discussion in chapter 4 of *Utilitarianism*, where he claims to supply a proof of the principle of utility, and also chapter 3 of Moore's *Principia Ethica* to see if Moore's criticism is fair.

In fact, few philosophers have followed Moore in holding that good is a simple, indefinable real property. However, many philosophers have been impressed by his formulations of the naturalistic fallacy and the open-question argument because they raise the issue of the relation between the moral and the non-moral in a highly focused manner.

Suppose we *do* define the fundamental moral value, and suppose we define it in non-moral terms. Imagine that we succeed in avoiding any appeal to evaluative terms in arriving at the definition and do not just trace out a definition in a moral circle. If we succeed at fashioning a definition, then we fail, because what the definition shows is that what we claimed was a fundamental moral value is really, ultimately, something non-moral (such as pleasure, or what is desired for its own sake, or happiness). If we define the moral in non-moral terms we effectively eliminate the moral, and show how it is analytically reducible to something else. If good is *nothing but* X (which is something non-moral) then haven't we dispensed with good as genuine moral value? How could we ask whether anything that is X or has X is good? However, as Moore says, "it may be always asked, with significance, of the complex so defined, whether it is itself good."[7]

Moore thought that the possibilities concerning the definability of "good" were as follows.

> In fact, if it is not the case that "good" denotes something simple and indefinable, only two alternatives are possible: either it is a complex, a given whole, about the correct analysis of which there may be disagreement; or else it means nothing at all, and there is no such subject as Ethics.[8]

The second of the alternatives is ruled out and the first is untenable. This is not to say that Moore thought that moral value had nothing to do with natural properties. He held that moral value *depends* upon the presence of non-moral properties. Something is good in virtue of its good-making properties, not in a random or mysterious way. Given that a thing has certain properties, it is necessary that it is a good thing. But good is not reducible to non-moral properties. For example, we might say that a social arrangement which is orderly and peaceful, and which facilitates the well being of those who participate in it, is a morally good social arrangement, though good is not simply equivalent to those properties by definition. It is morally good that a person have certain characteristics, among them honesty, conscientiousness, beneficence, and fairness. But good is not simply equivalent to those in a way that can be shown by a definition of good.

We shall now proceed to look at some of the main approaches in the debate about naturalism since Moore's time. Some of the most influential views are attempts to show that the best account of the dependence of the moral on the non-moral actually restores considerable plausibility to naturalism. Many recent theorists agree with Moore that moral value cannot be *defined* in naturalistic terms but they argue that it can be *explained* or accounted for in naturalistic terms. They argue that that the relation between non-moral and moral properties can be specified in ways Moore did not consider because the relation is not a strictly semantic one. Like Moore, they are making a case for the objectivity of moral value and for cognitivism with regard to moral judgment. However, they believe that moral value has naturalistic objectivity.

Reconstructed Naturalism

Theorists who want to avoid non-naturalism but who still want to maintain cognitivism argue that non-moral properties can (in some non-definitional way) determine or constitute moral properties. The aim is to preserve the reality of moral value while also preserving its relation to, and dependence upon, what is non-moral. (These are approaches of types (2), (3), and (4) indicated above.) We will look at one important approach to reconstructing naturalism in this section and at others in later sections of the chapter.

We begin by considering an analogy to a non-moral example, namely the relationship between the properties of hydrogen atoms and oxygen atoms on the one hand, and the property wetness (within a certain temperature range) on the other. When hydrogen and oxygen atoms combine in a certain way a distinct property (wetness) is present. A property that depends upon properties that are unlike it, but where they are found, it is found, is called a **supervenient** property. The base properties "fix" or determine the supervenient property. Wetness is a property of H_2O in a non-accidental way, but the relationship between wetness and the properties of hydrogen and oxygen is not strictly logical or definitional. There are laws of nature that explain the relationship, but they are empirically discovered. The relationship cannot be ascertained just by conceptual or linguistic analysis. Accounts in terms of supervenience appeal to naturalists because "What a naturalist wants is to be able to locate value, justice, right, wrong, and so forth in the world in the way that tables, colors, genes, temperatures, and so on can be located in the world."[9] That is to say, moral properties are real and the presence of moral properties depends, in very definite ways, upon the presence of certain non-moral properties. As David Brink has stated the view, "Naturalists claim that moral properties supervene on natural properties *because* moral properties are constituted by natural properties."[10] Wetness is real enough, and so is moral value. But each depends upon the presence and properties of something else.

This approach may supply a path for naturalism between Moore's non-naturalism on one side and the naturalistic fallacy and the open question argument on the other. If moral values supervene on natural facts and properties because they are constituted by them, then there is a specifiable, substantive, and necessary relation between them, and we need not regard moral value as non-natural.

Naturalists may want to make a claim stronger than the claim that moral values supervene on natural phenomena, and claim that they are *identical* with them. That is to say, moral values are not only realized by natural facts and properties, but there is no way in which they could be constituted or realized besides the way they in fact are – they just are identical with them, and are necessarily identical with them. Water (let us suppose), is identical with H_2O. That is, "water equals H_2O" is a true theoretical identity. That was discovered, and seeing that it is true is not simply a matter of knowing the meaning of the word "water." People used the term "water" meaningfully and correctly before they were in possession of the chemical theory according to which we now know that water is H_2O.

The identity thesis concerning moral value and natural properties (or concerning the relation between mind and brain, or aesthetic properties and natural properties, or other pairs of properties) is that moral value is identical with naturalistic phenomena, and that this is necessarily true, though it is not simply a truth of meaning (such as "a triangle is a three-sided enclosed figure"). We can discover identities in the process of inquiry and theorizing. They are necessary relations that cannot be ascertained just by considering the meanings of the terms involved. The identities are established by finding out that they are true. They are not definitional stipulations, but the result of a correct theory about what there is and what it is like.

The thesis of supervenience by constitution holds that moral values are realized by certain natural facts and properties, but that it is at least conceivable that they could be otherwise realized. The identity thesis is stronger than the constitution thesis, though both explicate moral value naturalistically, and both explicate the relation between the moral and the non-moral in terms other than semantic or conceptual necessity. Water is *identical* with H_2O, while wetness is a property *constituted* by the properties of H_2O but one that can also be constituted by other things.

Why doesn't Moore himself count as a naturalist of the supervenience-by-constitution sort? After all, he too held that moral values depend upon non-moral properties. Isn't that supervenience? Moore argued that good could not be defined in terms of other kinds of properties, and it could not be identical with them. He did not explicitly consider the H_2O—wetness type of model. (Similarly, a table is constituted of the wood out of which it is made, but is not definable in terms of it, and the wood is constituted by atoms of certain kinds, but not definable in terms of properties of them.) His focus throughout was on the definitional issue as though it was the only way to establish a necessary connection between properties. While he clearly made a case for dependence, it is not clear that we should interpret Moore's view as an instance of the theory of supervenience by constitution. He insists that good is *sui generis* (i.e. unique, of its own kind) and so it is likely that he would balk at regarding it as literally constituted by anything non-moral. His main concern seemed to be whether moral value has a real and distinct nature, though he approached the issue through a distinctively semantic test. He was quite clear about rejecting naturalism, and this was because he was convinced that *no moral property could just be or be constituted by a natural property* (or any other kind).

As we saw above, in recent theorizing there are accounts of moral value supervening on non-moral facts and properties that do not depend narrowly on semantic considerations. At the same time, Moore's work also motivated the search for alternatives to both naturalism and non-naturalism. We turn now to some of those approaches.

Non-cognitivist Alternatives

Two views that accepted Moore's critique of naturalism but rejected non-naturalism are **emotivism** and **prescriptivism**. Moore, emotivists, and prescriptivists agree that moral values cannot be completely explicated in naturalistic terms. They agree that the moral and the natural are distinct. Where emotivists and prescriptivists part company with Moore is over the issue of the objectivity and the realism of moral value. Emotivists and prescriptivists draw particular attention to the use of moral language. It is an important part of their view that in using moral language we are not reporting on moral properties. Instead, we are expressing attitudes or commitments, and also attempting to influence others' attitudes and commitments. When I say that murder is wrong I am showing that I have a certain stand and that I think that others should share it, I am not reporting that I have encountered a certain moral property or fact. Moral language looks like fact-stating language; the sentence "Murder is wrong" has the same surface grammar as "Dueling is dangerous." But in using the sentences the speaker is doing quite different things.

Part of the explanation of this, according to emotivists and prescriptivists, is that when we assert that courage is good or fairness is good, for example, those claims have both a descriptive component and an evaluative dimension. Courage and fairness are morally good; we are *for* them. That is the evaluative dimension. The descriptive component concerns what makes an act or a practice courageous or fair. We might say that courage is a certain kind of management of fear and a willingness to persist in the face of threat, risk, etc. Those are factual, and not evaluative, matters. Fairness involves addressing different persons' claims in ways that are not biased or arbitrary, and the like. That we approve of it is an evaluative matter. There are facts on the one hand, and there are stances and attitudes on the other. It is crucial not to conflate these. The evaluative dimension of moral language is not a matter of referring to moral reality, but a matter of what we do in using moral language. We express, we encourage, we discourage, we commend, and so forth. But we do not state moral facts or report on the presence of moral properties. Critics of naturalism also argue that a non-naturalist metaphysics and epistemology of value are hopelessly problematic and there is a satisfactory account of moral discourse, reasoning, and experience that involves no commitment to them. (Recall our discussion of subjectivism in chapter 1.)

A. J. Ayer, an influential emotivist theorist, wrote: "What we are interested in is the possibility of reducing the whole sphere of ethical terms to non-ethical terms. We are enquiring whether statements of ethical value can be translated into statements of empirical fact."[11] He goes on to argue that ethical concepts are unanalyzable; they *cannot* be translated into statements of empirical fact. However, in his view, this is because "they are mere pseudo-concepts. The presence of an ethical symbol in a proposition adds nothing to its factual content."[12] (Actually, Moore and his emotivist critics agree on the importance of semantic considerations, but draw different conclusions from them. Moore thought that there must be at least one unanalyzable ethical concept, and that it was a genuine concept.)

According to Ayer, in making ethical statements we are "merely expressing certain moral sentiments."[13] These sentiments matter to us, and we also care that others should agree with us and be moved by our moral responses and attitudes. Emotivists argue that neither naturalism nor non-naturalism can supply plausible accounts of the expressive function of moral judgments and the ways in which they influence, and are intended to influence, action. After all, moral judgment concerns what we should *do*. Moral judgments are practical because they express stances and attitudes. As we saw in chapter 1, the view that moral values are not objective may be "deflationary" metaphysics, but it need not amount to a denial of the importance of moral matters. Emotivists are supplying an account of moral language that shows that it does not refer to moral properties. But what we do with moral language is important because of the importance of moral matters.

Emotivism need not be understood to imply that just any feeling or stance is morally sound. We can speak of people's values being appropriate or inappropriate, subtle or unsubtle, informed or uninformed, and the like. We can also adjust, refine, and revise our moral judgments. When we are apprised of certain facts and when we see the ways in which others judge, we sometimes change our responses and judgments. Think, for example, of how a person with bigoted views might change them upon learning that various things he thought about a certain group simply are not true. Or a supporter of capital punishment might cease to support it upon learning that there is no conclusive evidence that it deters murderers, though this is not a matter of bringing a moral fact into view. It brings a fact into view, but not a moral fact. The emotivist interpretation of moral values is not that they have no relation to the facts, but that there are no moral facts, and that moral properties are not among what there is in the world.

Prescriptivism is a descendant of emotivism and shares some of its main elements. It denies that moral judgments report facts and that moral values can be interpreted in naturalistic terms. It also focuses on moral language and what we *do* in making moral claims. What it adds to the basic emotivist theses is the insistence that moral judgments express prescriptions, i.e. decisions or commitments about what to do that the agent *universalizes* so that they apply to all agents. The prescriptivist puts weight not only on the expressive dimension of moral judgment but also on its distinctive formal character, namely the way in which moral judgments are made with an intention to apply generally. Moral judgments, the prescriptivist insists, are intended to be more than personally expressive. They indicate the taking of a stand one is willing to universalize and a commitment to value one takes to be especially significant. We do not, for example, universalize judgments about fashion or culinary taste. In this way the prescriptivist draws particular attention to the practical, action-guiding function of moral judgments, their general prescriptive significance, and their priority over other kinds of potentially action-guiding considerations.

R. M. Hare, an important exponent of prescriptivism, remarks that moral judgments are "distinguished from other judgments of this class [the class of prescriptive judgments] by being universalizable."[14] For example, in making the judgment that deceitful promising is wrong, one is prescribing that deceitful promises are not to be made. This is quite different from the judgment "this stuff is awful" when you are talking about the taste of a food, or the color someone suggested to paint the house, or the judgment that icing on cakes should always be chocolate. There is no general prescriptive significance to those judgments, but there is in the judgment that kidnapping is wrong. Similarly, there is no general prescriptive significance to the judgment "you ought to get a calculus tutor," because there is only a reason to get one if you need and want to do better in calculus. It is not a prescription for everyone (in the way that "do not murder" is).

Hare argues that "what is wrong with naturalist theories is that they leave out the prescriptive or commendatory element in value-judgements, by seeking to make them derivable from statements of fact."[15] Like Ayer, he agrees with Moore's critique of naturalism but not with Moore's positive account. Both emotivism and prescriptivism are basically expressivist theories of moral judgment. Moore focused on what he took to be the entity or property to which "good" refers. His point was that moral value is real and objective and independent of what we happen to will or approve of or disapprove of. Thus, moral judgments state moral facts. Expressivists argue that the proper account of moral judgment focuses on what we are expressing and what we are doing in issuing moral judgments. They just do not refer to any moral facts or properties, and do not need to in order to be meaningful. Their meaning is not cognitive, fact-stating meaning – but that is not the only kind of meaning. There is also expressive meaning and it is relevant to action and valuative judgment.

Expressivist theories have been prominent during the past seventy or so years and continue to be refined and developed. An important aspect of them is that while they reject naturalism, they hold that there are important relations between non-moral facts and moral judgments. Simon Blackburn, for example, makes a crucial point about the consistency of moral judgments as follows: "Now it is not possible to hold an attitude to a thing because of its possessing certain properties and, at the same time, not hold that attitude to another thing that is believed to have the same properties."[16] Hare had made much the same point. Using the example of pictures in a gallery, Hare said:

> Suppose that either P is a replica of Q or Q of P, and we do not know which, but do know that both were painted by the same artist at about the same time. Now there is one thing that we cannot say; we cannot say "P is exactly like Q in all respects save this one, that P is a good picture and Q not." If we were to say this, we should invite the comment, "But how can one be good and the other not, if they are exactly alike? There must be some further difference between them to make one good and the other not."[17]

Consistency requires similar responses to similar situations, even though there is no objective value that we cognitively encounter, which is entailed by, identical with, or constituted by naturalistic facts and properties. There is a coherent general structure to moral judgments even though the judgments express responses or stances rather than report the detection of value. Every view we have discussed takes consistency and generality seriously. Moore and naturalists would also argue that where a complex of properties realizes some moral value, any exactly similar complex of properties must realize that moral value, though Moore thinks that value is real and has a distinct nature, and the naturalist thinks that value is either identical with or constituted by natural properties.

Given the emphasis prescriptivism puts on universalization and consistency it plainly assigns a role to rationality in moral judgment. But this role is an essentially formal one. This emphasis on universalization may remind you of a key element of Kant's moral theory. But the prescriptivist and Kant differ over whether one's moral principles reflect rational requirements (Kant) or choices and decisions (the prescriptivist). The universal imperative significance of moral judgments is grounded in their prescriptivity, not in requirements of pure practical reason.

While moral properties are not naturalistic they are related in regular, subject-dependent ways to non-moral properties. We can call this a theory of *subjective supervenience*. Above, we used the relation between H_2O and wetness to illustrate objective supervenience, the view that there are moral properties but they are identical with or constituted by non-moral properties. Subjective supervenience can be illustrated by considering how we might explicate the relation between sound waves and uncomfortable loudness. The differences between the two cases will highlight an important contrast between objective and subjective versions of supervenience.

In the case concerning sound, being uncomfortably loud (to us) depends in a regular way upon certain objective physical properties of sound waves but it is not itself a property of them. It is a property of how we respond to them. Being audible, we might say, supervenes on physical facts and on facts about us, but being *uncomfortably* loud supervenes subjectively, not objectively. Creatures with different thresholds of auditory discomfort find different sounds soothing, tolerable, or uncomfortable. When we say that a sound is uncomfortably loud, even if it is uncomfortably loud to the same degree for all of us, we are expressing a response to it, not noting a fact about the sound in its own right. The uncomfortable loudness is not an objective feature of the world, though it is certainly a feature of our experience of it.

In both models of supervenience there are connections between the moral and the non-moral, but the "location" of supervenience in each case is different. Also, in both models, *talk* of moral properties is in order though the naturalist takes that talk literally and the expressivist interprets it otherwise. The expressivist has no objection to saying that it is true that murder is wrong, but this is interpreted expressively rather than in cognitivist terms. It is all right to say that in the second model, value "comes from" us, as long as we remember that in this view there are regular relations between natural properties and moral values, and moral judgments are not haphazard or arbitrary. While one can give grounds for one's responses in terms of naturalistic features of what one is responding to (for example, we can say it was cruel because it was an unprovoked, malicious assault, and the attacker took pleasure in harming his victim), it would not be correct to say that moral values *just are* certain arrangements of non-moral properties.

In both objective and subjective supervenience the answer to the question "what is the relation between moral value and non-moral properties?" is "it depends," but the character of dependence is different in the two views. Expressivists argue that moral claims may be objective-looking in so far as we support them by various factual considerations. But there are no *moral* facts, and moral value has its source in us, as beings with a certain kind of sensibility with characteristic responses and concerns.

Hume and Naturalism

Accounts in terms of subjective supervenience are descendants of some Humean claims and arguments concerning moral value, modified by developments since Moore's time. An important development since then is the emphasis on various aspects of moral language. These descendants take over Hume's insistence that facts are facts, and our knowledge of them is not in itself action-guiding. They also take over Hume's insistence that there are coherent patterns to moral judgments even though those judgments do not report moral facts. They agree with Hume that moral facts or objective moral values are not needed in order for morality to be genuine and to have the authority in our lives that it seems to have. (Recall our discussion of this issue in chapter 1.)

We saw earlier that Hume held that we naturally have certain sentiments, propensities, and concerns, which shape our moral judgments. They are the engine and the fuel for the evaluation of actions, characters, and practices. Reason does not detect values. There are no values for reason to detect, and neither is reason a source of motivation. That is always a matter of desire or feeling. Nonetheless, as we noted, we refine, coordinate, and criticize our sentiments, and we can do so on the basis of factual beliefs. Hume wrote:

> But though reason, when fully assisted and improved, be sufficient to instruct us in the pernicious or useful tendency of qualities and actions; it is not alone sufficient to produce any moral blame or approbation. ... It is requisite a *sentiment* should here display itself, in order to give a preference to the useful above the pernicious tendencies. ... Here therefore *reason* instructs us in the several tendencies of actions, and humanity makes a distinction in favor of those which are useful and beneficial.[18]

One might object that if obligations, for example, are explained in terms of the projection of sentiments (subjective supervenience) rather than in terms of detection of moral facts, then obligations are somehow less than "the real thing." Blackburn, in defending an expressivist view, says that when one holds such a view, "he affirms *all that could ever properly be meant* by saying that there are real obligations"[19] (italics in original). We might put the point this way: human beings are naturally susceptible to morality. They naturally (presumably as a result of evolution) have a range of sentiments and propensities that are articulated into moral positions and judgments. There is no need for knowledge of a moral "reality" that has a standing independent of what humans feel and care about. Thus, we can call this naturalism at least in the broad sense that only naturalistic considerations are needed in order to account for moral value and moral judgment, though we are not *identifying* values with naturalistic facts or properties or claiming that the former are constituted by the latter. Moral valuing and behavior can be explained in terms of our natural propensities and the affective dimensions of our nature.

This is not to say that we are "naturally" moral in the sense of being naturally good, but to say that nothing non-naturalistic is needed to explain our involvement in morality. We naturally have some measure of concern for others and have a natural propensity for a measure of sociability. We can work out cooperative arrangements and strategies of mutual benefit. There are significant gains to us in cooperation, mutual assistance, and acting in rule-governed ways. We can explain the source and basis of moral values and judgments by reference to naturalistic features of human beings.

The kind of naturalism we discussed earlier, according to which moral values are constituted by natural facts and properties, is an attempt to save moral objectivity without non-naturalism. It is meant to show how moral judgments are cognitive judgments that are literally true or false. Humean naturalism also avoids non-naturalism but without treating moral values as objective. It is, we might say, skeptical naturalism, in contrast to realist naturalism. According to Hume's view, factual judgments are fully cognitive. Moral judgments are not. Factual judgments report what is the case. Moral judgments do not. Factual judgments are not action-guiding. Moral judgments are. These are all ways in which the view depends upon a distinction between facts and values. Theories of moral value that borrow extensively from Hume do not attempt to put moral value on a basis of naturalistic realism, though they are naturalistic in what they *deny* and in what they appeal to in their accounts of moral phenomena. They are skeptical about objective values, but not about morality. As we saw in chapter 1, it is important to see that metaethical arguments denying the objectivity of moral value need not be intended to diminish morality and the significance of moral claims. Often, their point is to give an account of moral language and moral judgments.

Reconnecting Facts and Values

Since Moore's time the meaning and use of moral language have been a focus of a great deal of the most important work. For several decades after the publication of Moore's *Principia Ethica* in 1903 the view that descriptive meaning and evaluative meaning are distinct was widely and confidently held. It seemed to many philosophers that cognitivist accounts of moral value could not make sense of the practical dimensions of ethical discourse and judgment. They argued for a distinction between the expressive and action-guiding features of the use of moral language on the one hand, and the fact-stating, descriptive use of language on the other. Indeed, a distinction between fact and value is part of the way many people understand moral value independently of having a philosophical theory. It is widely held that facts are objective and values are subjective – that factual statements are either true or false, and that moral statements reflect attitudes, personal commitments, or stances that do not report facts. However, the distinctions between fact and value, and between factual meaning and evaluative meaning, have come under considerable critical scrutiny during the past few decades.

We should consider some of the doubts about whether there is a clean break between descriptive meaning and evaluative meaning. A closely related point is that moral evaluation needs to be understood in terms of being suited to, proper to, or merited by the facts. For example, if we have a clear and accurate conception of what courage is and what fairness is, there is not then an independent matter of how to evaluate them. There is not a purely descriptive meaning and then an evaluative laminate that we express toward it or project onto it. We understand that courage and fairness merit endorsement because of the ways in which they are good, rather than their goodness being based on our approval of them or expression of a positive stance toward them. Perhaps, then, there is an interpenetration of the factual and the valuative in a way that does not distill them out from each other in pure and separate forms.

Philippa Foot is one of the key figures in criticizing the distinction between fact and value. She was an early and important critic of emotivism and prescriptivism. They were very much in ascendance in the 1950s and 1960s when she wrote some of her most influential articles. In her view:

> The crucial question is this. Is it possible to extract from the meaning of words such as "good" some element called "evaluative meaning" which we can think of as externally related to its objects? Such an element would be represented, for instance, in the rule that when any action was "commended" the speaker must hold himself bound to accept an imperative "let me do these things."[20]

That's what prescriptivism would say. Foot went on:

> I wish to say that this hypothesis is untenable, and that there is no describing the evaluative meaning of "good," evaluation, commending, or anything of the sort, without fixing the object to which they are supposed to be attached. Without first laying hands on the proper object of such things as evaluation, we shall catch in our net either something quite different such as accepting an order or making a resolution, or else nothing at all.[21]

Foot argued that separating out evaluative meaning in the manner of most critiques of naturalism distorts and misrepresents the concepts we use in making moral judgments. Could a person understand what fairness, benevolence, or honesty is without also understanding that each of these is morally good? Can we really specify the contents of these concepts and then ask a *separate* question about our stance or attitude toward those contents? (Is it an open question in *that* way?) Is moral judgment a matter of choice or decision in that way? Can the facts "take" or "accept" just any stance, or do they seem to have a certain kind of moral significance in their own right? What looked like a very plausible move, the move that told us that there is something inscrutable and strange about moral facts, now looks as though it is based upon a contrived and distorting distinction. It is not just that similar facts require similar responses as a matter of consistency. In addition, moral judgments are made on the basis of our understanding of the facts.

Critics of expressivism argue that while acting morally involves commitment and choice, it does not involve *decision* about what has value in the way that at least some versions of the fact–value distinction indicate. We have to decide what to do, but that is a different role for decision. Value is more closely related to fact than emotivism and prescriptivism suggest. Moral choice and commitment can themselves be guided by comprehension of the moral significance of facts. They are more cognitive and less purely volitional than the fact–value distinction suggests. Granted, complex and difficult issues remain about whether, for example, it is ever morally permissible to be dishonest, or what courage requires in a certain situation. But these are not questions about where descriptive meaning ends and evaluative meaning begins. They are questions to be settled by hard, ongoing moral thought and reflection upon experience, not by sorting meanings into a descriptive bin and an evaluative bin.

This sort of response to emotivism and prescriptivism did not come onto the scene as a direct defense of naturalism, but it should be clear how it could play a role in defense of it. It is a way of showing how the most plausible interpretation of moral concepts and judgments reveals how objective value considerations are ineliminable from those concepts and judgments. Attitudes, stances, and responses can themselves be examined, criticized, and revised in light of factual considerations. This shows, it is held, that moral value is no worse off, in terms of being objective, than many other things. Horses are mammals and cruelty is wrong; in each case, full credentials for objectivity are met. When we use moral concepts, we are using concepts to think about moral issues, but we are using concepts cognitively and not in a fundamentally different way from how we use non-moral concepts. Moral concepts are not pseudo-concepts.

For example, the person who thinks degradation or cruelty is morally permissible lacks sound moral comprehension. That agent fails to understand something correctly. The wrongness of his view is not just a matter of his having an unwelcome attitude or his being out of step with the prevailing norms. The suggestion that cruelty could be permissible if one finds it to be so seems to be not just morally obnoxious but conceptually confused. Moral evaluation is to be interpreted as a rational response to the normative significance of factual considerations. If there really is a clean break between fact and value then there is no answer (in terms of cognitive considerations) to the question "*Why* prescribe this instead of that?" Ultimately, on expressivist terms, moral judgments are not based upon objective considerations of value.

They reflect decisions or attitudes. Expressivists can insist that moral stances respond to facts and must be consistent. But is that sufficient to disallow the possibility that on their terms, cruelty cannot be morally permissible?

Critics of expressivism do not deny that there is indeed a role for sensibility in the account of morality. Of course, feeling and desire have a role in moral judgment and motivation, but not a role that is cleanly separable from the role of cognition. It is a role *in those*, and not a role confined to projecting qualities onto things in the world or confined to expression. (Discussions in earlier chapters should suggest to you that there is often a good deal of Aristotelian resonance in this sort of view. We will say more about this below.) Recalling our earlier examples, we should say that the property of being uncomfortably loud is projected; the property of being morally wrong or morally wrong *because* dishonest and malicious is not.

In order to explain this, it might be helpful to consider an analogy to the case of sense perception. Fresh tomato sauce is red, and the judgment that it is red depends upon our perceptual sensibility – but it *is* red, and that is what accurate perception tells us. In the perceptual case there are roles for the objective circumstances; facts about the object of perception and the conditions of perception. And there is a role for the subjectivity of the perceiver; the way we experience objects through the senses depends upon peculiarly human modes of perception and the way in which the capacities for them operate in certain conditions.

Perhaps there are reasons to think that the red of a ripe tomato *as experienced* is not an exact copy of the features of the tomato that cause us to see it as red. Those features are described by physical theory as certain structures and arrangements, and not in terms of color as it visually appears. There are law-like causal relations between physical structure and appearance, but that does not mean that what causes it to look a certain way is in the tomato in exactly the way that we experience it. This might seem to be a point in favor of the critique of naturalism. The counterpart in the moral context would be that moral evaluation is a kind of "coloring" we attribute to things, but it really "comes from" us, and moral value is not objectively "out there."

However, let us look at the color of the tomato from another angle. Consider the issue of color in the following way, suggested by John McDowell. That it is:

a property the ascription of which to an object is not adequately under-stood except as true, if it is true, in virtue of the object's disposition to present a certain sort of perceptual appearance: specifically, an appear-ance characterizable by using a word for the property itself to say how the object perceptually appears. Thus an object's being red is under-stood as obtaining in virtue of the object's being such (in certain cir-cumstances) to look, precisely, red.[22]

His point is that in our experience of color in the typical cases, we have good reason to take the perceptual awareness of properties as the "perceptual awareness of properties genuinely possessed by the objects that confront one."[23] The objectivity of the tomato's being red is not in doubt, though the way in which we experience its color is of course affected by our having the sort of perceptual capacities we have.

McDowell did not intend this to be an exact analogy to the moral case. He was not arguing that the claim that cruelty is wrong is to be explained in just the same way as the claim that the ripe tomato is red. He notes that in the moral context the issue is whether judgments are *merited* by their objects, rather than causally explained by them, as in the perceptual case. But the abstract point of similarity in the two cases is that in both cases it is objective properties that "validate the re-sponses."[24] (You might try to explicate the differences between this approach and accounts in terms of subjective supervenience.) In nei-ther context is the judgment of the presence of the property a matter that is based upon projecting subjective responses onto the world and mistakenly regarding them as "out there" when they are grounded in nothing more than features internal to our experience.

In some of his more recent work, McDowell suggests that maybe the best way to understand the relation between objective features of things and our responses is that *neither* side (neither the world nor our re-sponses) has clear priority. McDowell calls this the "no-priority" view. "If there is no comprehending the right sentiments independently of the concepts of the relevant extra features, a no-priority view is surely indicated."[25] A non-moral example McDowell uses is what makes some-thing funny. Neither our laughing, nor our inclination to laugh, is what makes something funny. There are things that people laugh at, which are not funny. There are funny things that people do not laugh at. We cannot explicate what it is to be funny just in terms of project-ing a response or an attitude, or just in terms of what response is elicited. The response or the attitude is apt, or is well placed on the basis of what it takes as its objects. The humor in something is something about *it*, and sometimes on account of our understanding being enlarged or our becoming informed, we can "see" the humor in something, or see that there is no humor in it. A situation may seem very funny until we learn more facts about it. Someone who still thinks it is funny has a perverse or childish sense of humor.

Perhaps humor is not the best case. It appears to be especially suited for a subjectivist reading. It may seem that we have reason to conclude that there is no such thing as a sense of humor in anything like the way there is a sense of sight or hearing, in that what is funny is a matter of personal taste, cultural norms, and other factors that show that it is not objective. A person's sense of humor may be out of step with others', but that does not show that it is defective or that his judgments of what is funny are mistaken. But then, consider matters such as being admirable, or despicable, or worthy of gratitude. These are hardly matters of individual taste or disposition, though sentiments are involved in correctly recognizing what is admirable, despicable, or worthy of gratitude. They are good examples of how neither objective facts nor subjective attitudes and responses exclusively determine or constitute moral values. Certain responses are correct and can be supported with reasons. We learn how to apply these concepts, and what makes the feelings appropriate by understanding various facts about agents, actions, and situations. The person who has done you a good turn, for the sake of your own good, is a person to whom gratitude is owed. This is not true of the person who did something for you in a mainly self-seeking way. The facts and the values, the cognitive and the evaluative, are not altogether distinct from each other or analytically separable.

We remarked at the outset that naturalism itself is open to various interpretations, and we have looked at a number of them. Some give an account of moral values as constituted by or identical with non-moral properties. The Humean view focuses on sentiments and concerns that are natural to human beings and are the basis for projecting value in certain ways. It is fair to also regard views like Foot's and McDowell's as examples of naturalism. They are non-Platonic and non-Kantian, but are cognitivist and objectivist. They do not attempt to show the relation of moral properties to non-moral properties in a manner analogous to attempts to show that biological properties can be reduced to, or supervenient upon physio-chemical properties, but they argue that correct understanding and use of moral concepts involves grasping the objective moral significance of facts. Some of the main features of this view are the following.

1 There is not the distinction between fact and value, and between description and evaluation, that was central to many critiques of naturalism.
2 There are roles for sensibility and cognition in moral judgment, but the role of sensibility does not undermine the objectivity of moral judgment.
3 Given the way in which moral judgments are objective, it is appropriate to regard them as being literally true or false.
4 The objectivity of moral judgment is not a matter of theoretically relating moral values to natural facts and properties. It is indicated by the way in which reflection reveals what is involved in understanding moral concepts, judgments, and the semantics of moral discourse.

Aristotle and Naturalism

Recent debates about the nature of moral judgment and moral reasoning have their roots deep in the history of philosophy. For example, Hare and Blackburn owe a great deal to Hume. Foot and McDowell owe a great deal to Aristotle. Each approach seeks to avoid commitment to a non-natural ontology, and each seeks to avoid reductively analyzing moral value in non-moral terms. The more Aristotelian views, in contrast to the more Humean views, argue the case for moral cognitivism and realism. However, they are not versions of teleological perfectionism as was Aristotle's theory. That is to say, they are not embedded in a background conception of what is the best life for a human being, which is itself based upon a conception of the realization of a human essence. Rather, they develop resources in Aristotle's philosophy in their accounts of moral cognition and judgment. What these recent views take over from Aristotle is the emphasis on the importance of character, and in particular the virtues, to moral judgment and reasoning, without also interpreting the virtues as excellences that perfect human nature. We need to say a bit more about this and then ask if a theory in which the virtues are central can be successfully elaborated without a background commitment to the sort of teleological metaphysics Aristotle endorsed.

Aristotle's conception of nature overall was a normative one, in that he held that for any given natural kind (say, bovine, equine, human) there is, for members of that kind, a condition of successful actualization or realization of their nature. The physiology of a healthy oak is ordered in a way that enables the plant to flourish in the manner proper to oaks. A diseased oak, or an oak damaged by drought, fails to fully actualize its nature. There are goods appropriate to it according to its nature. Similarly with respect to a dog or fish or human being, or any other organism. A human being, though, has the capacity to pursue and actualize its good through deliberate activity, through reasoning and choice. In leading a human life the individual fashions and enacts conceptions of its good. The life-activity of a human being does not just go successfully or unsuccessfully "anyway" as a result of innate natural tendencies and environmental conditions. That is how the life of an oak or a fish is lived. They do not and cannot conceptualize their goods and then strive to actualize those conceptions. They do well or badly *simply* by nature and circumstance.

Of course, conditions we cannot control also make a difference to whether we live well or badly. But according to Aristotle, the core of whether we flourish or not is a matter of how we exercise capacities for voluntary activity, and that exercise centrally involves reason's role in comprehending goods and guiding action by deliberation. If we lead excellent lives it is largely to our credit as voluntary agents. If we lead lives that merit censure and criticism then that too is typically something for which we are accountable. The virtues of character that enable us to act well involve both affect and cognition. Unless we have the emotions and desires that make us sensitive to valuative matters in the appropriate ways we will not be able to judge actions and situations correctly and we will not deliberate well about them. Similarly, our emotions and desires are not "blind" but need to be guided by cognitive abilities so that we can discern and comprehend the significance of situations and actions. The excellent person has feelings and desires aligned with what reason understands to be good.

Aristotle says that "virtues are concerned with actions and feelings; but every feeling and every action implies pleasure or pain; hence, for this reason too, virtue is concerned with pleasures and pains."[26] In that respect, sensibility is crucial. We need proper sensibility in order to desire and enjoy what is genuinely good. He also says that the virtuous agent needs intelligence, which is a "state grasping the truth, involving reason, concerned with action about what is good or bad for a human being."[27] In that respect, understanding is crucial. "The unconditionally good deliberator is the one whose aim expresses rational calculation in pursuit of the best good for a human being that is achievable in action."[28] This is part of his view that "virtue makes the goal correct, and intelligence makes what promotes the goal [correct]."[29] This person judges, deliberates, and acts accordingly, with the feelings, desires, and responses appropriate to the value of things. The virtuous person feels and is moved by things in the right way, and that depends upon having good judgment and a perceptive understanding of situations.

A critic might insist that Aristotle has failed to make appropriate distinctions between natural facts and values, and between evaluative states of mind and cognitive ones. However, we can also see his view as recognizing the way in which desires and emotions, for example, involve beliefs (e.g. you are angry because you believe you have been slighted, you want to travel to Scotland because you believe it is a beautiful country, you feel gratitude because you know that someone has done you a service). Our receptivity and sensibility enable us to discriminate morally relevant features of actions and situations. For instance, compassion is not just a feeling of sympathy, it is also a way of acknowledging that certain types of regard for, or treatment of, others is in order. There is proper compassion and there is misdirected warmth, or a general, undifferentiated susceptibility to being moved by the suffering of others. Being compassionate in a morally sound manner involves judgment as well as feeling. Similarly, one can feel and show anger in morally proper or improper ways. Often, anger can be rationally justified, and the virtuous person feels anger in the right way, and his sensibility enables him to detect when anger is appropriate. As we all know, people can feel and express anger in all sorts of morally unsound ways, hurting others and themselves along the way. We nurse resentments; we trap undischarged anger and then discharge it at the wrong person; we are overly sensitive and become disproportionately angry; or we are too timid and do not become sufficiently angry and stand up for ourselves. This interpenetration of the cognitive and the valuative has been reconstructed by some recent metaethicists who are critical of the fact—value distinction in many of its formulations. If we possess the appropriate concepts and have learned the requisite types of perception and discernment, we can make correct moral judgments.

Though he did not attempt to theoretically identify moral value with non-moral facts, or provide an account of supervenience, Aristotle developed a view in which we find moral significance in the facts, acts, and situations we encounter in the natural world. Thus, for all of its differences from say, Mill's view, or Hume's views, Aristotle's can also be said to be a type of ethical naturalism because moral value does not have its source in pure reason or in divine command or a supernatural realm. The natures of things are the basis for judgments about what is their good and, accordingly, there are objective goods proper to human nature.

It has often been argued that a view of this kind can only seem plausible if we cling to a no longer credible teleological view of nature. We know now, it is claimed, that there is no intrinsic teleology in nature and that the grounds for ethical value cannot be found in a conception of human flourishing grounded in the "proper" ends for a human being. While it is true that human beings set ends, act purposively, conceive their lives in terms of values and ideals, and the like, there is no metaphysical or objective basis for a privileged conception of what it is to successfully actualize human nature. The view that there is seems unscientific and irreconcilable with what we understand about nature. There are laws of nature, but they describe what happens in nature and do not have any intrinsic ethical significance. There are no norms or values "built into" nature.

Thus, the question of what is a good life or the best life for a human being is not answered in terms of a conception of the proper operation of human capacities. Recall Williams's criticism of Aristotle, which was quoted in chapter 3. Or, rather, there are many different conceptions of what it is to live well that can plausibly claim to be grounded in the operation of human capacities. Guiding ideals, notions of what is worthwhile, commitments regarding the central concerns of a human life – these are diverse and there is no privileged formulation of them in terms of the essential properties of human nature.[30] There are many different human goods, many different ways of balancing and integrating them into good lives.

Even in light of skeptical considerations about whether there is a best kind of life for human beings, there has been a steady increase in efforts to develop Aristotle's insights and arguments in recent decades. Among these elements of his view are: (a) his notion of the virtues (as excellences of character needed in order to judge and act well); (b) his interpretation of the agreement of reason and desire (as the way in which cognitive and non-cognitive capacities are involved in ethical judgment and activity); and (c) the distinction between good and bad pleasures (reflecting distinctions between what merits being enjoyed and what is found pleasing though not properly choiceworthy). These elements of Aristotelian moral psychology and moral epistemology may well have a standing independent of Aristotle's teleological metaphysics.

Pursuing this direction in moral theorizing may lead to a reconstruction of elements of a teleological conception of human nature. If it does, it will do so through reflection upon moral discourse, judgments, and experience rather than as part of a "global" teleological metaphysics. We noted earlier that Aristotle was not addressing quite the same concern as, say, Kant or Mill. He was not seeking to identify the fundamental principle of right action, but showing how the exercise of practical reason is crucial to enabling a human being to lead a flourishing or excellent life. The idea that in order to lead such a life one must have certain guiding concerns with regard to action and have certain enduring states of character (the virtues) in order to enact those concerns has been restored as an important way of understanding moral judgment and action. The understanding of human action, the rational structure of a life overall, and the way in which cognition and feeling are interrelated may lead us to take teleological notions seriously even though we have abandoned Aristotle's overall conception of nature and the cosmos.

Moral Facts and Explanation

We have looked at a number of the main lines of debate concerning the relations between moral values and natural facts, and also at different conceptions of naturalism. In addition to these debates about how moral value is related to various kinds of facts, there is also a debate about whether we should be committed to moral facts because they have a role in *explaining* actions and judgments. An influential general philosophical view is that the best reason for thinking that a certain type of fact exists is that it is necessary for an adequate account of some range of phenomena and experience. That is why there is good reason to believe there are facts about oak trees, planets, electrical charges, and genes, but not about leprechauns, intergalactic travelers, and demonic possession, for example. If certain facts do no essential explanatory work, what support is there for regarding them as part of what there is? We do *not* need facts about demons or spirit-beings in order to explain the behavior of schizophrenics or epileptics. We *do* need to be committed to the existence of facts about genes as part of the best explanation of the inheritance of characteristics. Do we need moral facts in order to explain moral actions and judgments in anything like the way we need the facts of genetics to explain inheritance of traits, protein synthesis, and other biological and chemical phenomena? If we make no commitment to moral facts, is that costly with respect to our ability to explain other things?

A number of recent philosophers have answered "no." A particularly powerful strategy for raising doubts about moral facts is to argue that *even if* there were objective values or moral facts, they would be irrelevant to actual moral experience and practice. This is a way of giving the opponent his best case and showing that it is still untenable: at best, moral facts are superfluous, unnecessary for accounting for moral experience and judgment. Apart from whatever ontological and epistemological difficulties they bring with them in their own right, they are simply not needed.

Gilbert Harman has argued in this way. He writes:

> The observation of an event can provide observational evidence for or against a scientific theory in the sense that the truth of that observation can be relevant to a reasonable explanation of why that observation was made. A moral observation does not seem, in the same sense, to be observational evidence for or against any moral theory, since the truth or falsity of the moral observation seems to be completely irrelevant to any reasonable explanation of why that observation was made.[31]

Why is that? Because in order to explain the moral judgments people make:

> It would seem that all we need assume is that you have more or less well articulated moral principles that are reflected in the judgments you make, based on your moral sensibility. It seems to be completely irrelevant to our explanation whether your intuitive immediate judgment is true or false.[32]

In order to explain moral judgments or observations we do not need to posit moral facts. All of the resources needed for an adequate explanation of judgments and observations are supplied by two kinds of facts: facts about the psychology of the agents who make the judgments and non-moral facts about the world. Moral facts would be an explanatorily idle accessory. This, anyway, is Harman's view. We do not need a distinctive category of moral facts, including the fact that cruelty is wrong, that fairness is obligatory, that compassion is good, in order to explain the moral judgments we make and the actions we perform.

In critically discussing Harman's view, Nicholas Sturgeon writes:

> His claim is not that if the action had not been one of deliberate cruelty (or had otherwise differed in whatever way would be required to remove its wrongness), you would still have thought it wrong. It is, instead, that if the action were one of deliberate, pointless cruelty, but this did not make it wrong, you would still have thought it was wrong.[33]

In Harman's view this is because the only facts that are needed in order to explain your thinking the act is wrong are facts about your moral sensibility and the moral principles you are committed to. Those are enough. It is not the presence of the property *morally wrong* or the fact that an action is morally wrong that explains your judgment that it is wrong. In examining this argument, Sturgeon responds in a couple of ways. One is to argue that we regularly appeal to moral facts to explain judgments and actions, and that those facts are no more suspect than the facts we are committed to in other areas of inquiry and theorizing.

Defenders of moral facts insist that they do indeed have an important explanatory role, even in explaining certain non-moral phenomena. How else are we to explain Hitler's actions but in terms of the moral fact of his being depraved? Surely, the fact that Hitler was depraved is an element of the best explanation of what he did, why he thought it was the right thing to do, and why we find it unacceptable and horrible. Is it plausible (or even conceivable) that he would have done what he did if he were not depraved? Moral facts *are* explanatorily relevant, and if we dispense with them, doing so does not leave the situation where it was. If we abandon a commitment to them that would be comparable to arguing "that if Hitler's psychology, and anything else about his situation that could strike us as morally relevant, had been exactly as it in fact was, but this had not constituted moral depravity, he would still have done exactly what he did."[34] Recall that Harman's claim was about what is needed in order to *explain* moral observations and beliefs. Sturgeon points out that if no moral facts are needed to explain moral judgments, then presumably they are not needed to explain behavior, the very behavior that is morally judged. That, he argues, is quite implausible.

Harman claims that if there is no need to refer to moral facts in giving moral explanations then the question of whether there are moral facts and the debates about their metaphysical nature would be largely beside the point. Moral realists such as Sturgeon argue that we cannot "suspend" the metaphysical and epistemological issues, and that we need to posit certain moral facts in order to make sense of other facts. For example, the fact that a person is virtuous may well be part of the explanation of why he is held in high esteem and asked or elected to fill positions of responsibility or authority. The fact that a social and economic arrangement is just may well be part of the explanation of why it is stable and people have an interest in sustaining it. Far from being unneeded, moral facts are a familiar and essential part of our understanding of the world. The main issue is not whether they have some peculiar nature of their own but whether our best understanding of the world (including various kinds of facts, acts, and situations) involves reference to moral facts. Without reference to them, various important kinds of phenomena would not be satisfactorily explained.

How do moral facts "fit" into the world? How can there be facts about what is morally *obligatory* as well as facts about *what is the case*? Peter Railton argues that because they supervene on natural phenomena there is nothing metaphysically suspect about moral facts. He writes:

> Where is the place in explanation for facts about what *ought* to be the case – don't facts about the way things are do all the explaining there is to be done? Of course they do. But then, my naturalistic moral realism commits me to the view that facts about what ought to be the case are facts of a special kind about the way things are.[35]

He says, "In the spirit of a naturalized moral epistemology, we may ask whether the explanation of why we make certain moral judgments is an example of a reliable process for discovering moral facts."[36] Think, for example, about why there is such a high degree of consensus on the rejection of trial by ordeal as morally wrong. Aren't there facts about what is in people's interests, about what are appropriate and effective ways of gathering evidence and examining witnesses, and about what are rational strategies of belief-formation and acceptance, which are the basis for the moral fact that trial by ordeal is both cruel and wrong? We ought not to torture people to ascertain guilt or innocence. Why should we treat that as less than a fact?

Clearly, many different hypotheses are possible concerning what is needed to best explain moral experience and moral judgment. Plato thought that the form of the good was needed. Aristotle thought an intrinsic end for human nature was needed. Hume thought that a common human sensibility was needed. Ayer thought that examination of moral language showed moral concepts to be non-cognitive and showed that moral language had only expressive meaning. And so forth. Does the best account involve commitment to moral facts? Are they naturalistic moral facts? If they are, what is the best account of the way in which they are? As a philosophical method, the approach through the best explanation is, in its own right, open with respect to the metaphysics of morals. We can see that in the disagreement between Harman on the one hand and Sturgeon and Railton on the other. It might lead one to agree with Moore, and it might lead one to deny that there are moral facts of any kind, naturalistic or not. The idiom of "best explanation" is relatively recent, but it is a strategy that is to some extent at least implicit in many of the approaches we have examined. They are all concerned with how to best account for the facts of moral experience, thought, and practice, and how they are related to other kinds of facts. The approach of examining what is required for the best explanation is an attempt to answer the question "what is there?" by looking at the concepts, theories, and explanatory strategies that are essential to giving an account of some range of phenomena.

What about God?

We have looked at many of the main issues in the debate about the relation between moral values and natural facts and properties, but we have not yet said anything about theistic conceptions of moral value and moral requirements. Such views are both historically and philosophically important. Theism is an important type of non-naturalism that differs from the non-naturalistic views developed by Plato, Kant, and Moore. It raises a number of issues in addition to the ones we have already encountered. One issue concerns the way in which the notion of divine command is at the center of theistic morality.

It is important to guard against misrepresenting a morality of divine command. It is easy to portray religious morality as mainly *prudential* and as involving a kind of metaphysical intimidation: if you obey you will be rewarded and if you do not you will be punished. A religion-based morality is not simply prudential in that sense and, anyway, religion is not needed to underwrite prudence. Generally, religious traditions share the notion that faith and obedience to God are most perfect when they are ways of loving and trusting God. According to religious tradition there is an incalculable, non-natural good possible for us. This is union with God, or blessedness. However, the reason to be moral is not that we will get a big payoff in the end. The central idea is that there are moral values with a ground and source outside of us in God, whose commands are moral laws. In answering to God's authority we are answering to true values and fully authoritative commands. Moral value's objectivity transcends nature and reason and is made known to us by revelation. Also, the end that is possible for us is possible only through responding to what God has commanded. Again, this is not primarily a matter of prudence. It is a matter of responding to truth about good and an authority that can be unconditionally trusted and is to be unconditionally obeyed. It is true that in some religious traditions fear of divine punishment plays an important role. God has knowledge of all of our sins and does not leave them unpunished, and the punishment can be very terrible. Still, the fear of God and God's power to punish is acknowledgement of God as the supreme power and as the source of all value and obligation. It is not like fear of a despotic power, unconcerned with the good of those over whom it has power.

There are secular moral theories in which the notion of command is important. For example, Kant takes the notion of a command of reason to be essential to morality. But the moral law and its bindingness have their source in one's own reason and that is a crucial contrast with religious morality. Theistic morality also contrasts with an Aristotelian account. In the latter, there are objective excellences it is rational to acquire in order to realize human perfection, but there is no role for a God who has a providential plan for the world and who enables us to achieve perfections that transcend nature. The ways in which command and teleology figure in theistic morality differ from the ways in which they are found in Kant's and Aristotle's theories. God's power and God's plan for the world fundamentally alter the way in which morality is conceived.

To the critic of religion-based morality the involvement of divine command can look like an abdication of moral thought and submission to an external authority. To the defender of it, divine command is what guarantees the rightness and the bindingness of moral require-ments. According to the theist, it is the wisdom and power of God that supply the only adequate ground for the categorical requirements of morality and the only fully adequate guarantee of their rightness. Subjectivist or naturalistic accounts of moral value and moral obliga-tion could explain why we care about certain matters or why we believe there are reasons for us to act in certain ways. However, the theist would argue that they could not explain moral value and moral obligation as having an unconditional, non-contingent claim on us. Values and obligations interpreted naturalistically or in subjectivist terms would have a claim on us only in so far as *we* have a concern to be engaged to them. If value and obligation come from God, then (a) there is no question of their rightness, (b) they are aspects of the divine governance of the world and not merely objects of human concern, and (c) as such, they are crucial to the possibility of the non-natural perfection of human beings. They have a claim on us that is non-optional and is beyond question with regard to its authority.

Critics argue that if theistic morality's requirements are rationally supportable then there is no special need for them to have a religious basis. The reasons for them should be discernible and moral duties should be justifiable independent of divine command. If the reasons for God's commands are not independently justified, then it seems we are submitting ourselves to arbitrary will. This issue is explored in classic fashion in Plato's dialogue, *Euthyphro*. In the dialogue, which is about the nature of piety, Socrates says to Euthyphro, "Consider this: Is the pious loved by the gods because it is pious, or is it pious because it is loved by the gods?"[37] This is a powerful and succinct way of raising the question of whether God responds to what is good and right in its own nature, and wills commands in accord with it, or whether it is God's willing something that makes it right and obliga-tory. (Kant also takes this up, and says that "Even the Holy One of the Gospel must be compared with our [rational] ideal of moral perfection before He is recognized as such".[38]) Either what God commands can be rationally vindicated, or, in submitting to God's commands, we are submitting to an arbitrary will – and God could command us to do things that are awful. Either horn of the dilemma seems to seriously threaten a morality of divine command.

The theist might reply by arguing for the following claims. First, much of what is divinely commanded can be seen by us to be rational and morally required. That means not that it is right wholly independent of God, but that we can often understand the rightness of what God commands. Second, given the divine nature – that is, given what God *is* – God would only command what is right. Again, this does not imply that what is right or good is independent of God and that God reliably wills in accord with it. It means that a perfect being could not fail to command perfectly. As a result, we can see that, third, whatever God commands is right, *even if* we cannot always ascertain the way in which it is. (There may be moral requirements for which we cannot ascertain the rationale, as is the case for various ritual laws. But for many requirements, and many of the most basic ones, we *can* understand the rationale.) The theist needs to show that while moral laws have their source in divine command, that is not to say that God can make just anything morally required and morally good by commanding it. That is the crux of one of the most difficult and enduring problems of theistic ethics.

In some traditions an important relation is explicitly acknowledged between the theistic source of (many) moral commands and human reason. Our knowledge of morality is not exclusively a matter of what is revealed. A good example of this is the natural law approach as represented by Thomas Aquinas in the Catholic tradition. Of law in general he says that it "is nothing else than an ordinance of reason for the common good, promulgated by him who has the care of the community."[39] And "The natural law is promulgated by the very fact that God instilled it into man's mind so as to be known by him naturally."[40] Thus, natural law is accessible to all agents, whether or not they are theists. There are certain principles of practical reason that are knowable by all agents. Aquinas, of course, insists that God is the origin of natural law, and that natural law is the "participation of the eternal law in the rational creature"[41] but one need not believe in God or God's eternal law to see what is required by natural law. (Eternal law is God's providential plan for the world, the overall governance of the world by God.)

The theist might argue that even those who do not believe in God have some knowledge of God's law just by virtue of having moral understanding. For example, the atheist may assert that causing harm just for pleasure is of course always morally wrong, but deny that this is because God made this known to everyone through natural law. In fact, the atheist may deny that this is *knowledge*; he may claim it is just a stance or a personal commitment, and that in fact *no one* has moral knowledge. He is committed to it as an important part of morality but denies that it is a cognitive matter. The theist will interpret the stance or commitment as awareness of a law that is promulgated by God.[42] There can be knowledge even where it is not recognized as such. The atheist is confused (or obdurate) about the status of his moral beliefs, but he has correct ones in so far as we are beneficiaries of divine guidance – especially in respect of strict prohibitions, such as the wrongness of harming for fun. It is never right to do that, and *everyone* knows that, even if some deny that it is a cognitive matter.

Given this, the theist need not be committed to the view that the atheist cannot be morally good or cannot have moral knowledge. Perhaps through conscience or natural law a great deal of moral knowledge is available to rational agents whether or not they are theists. There will, of course, still be a difference between the theist and atheist over what ultimately underwrites moral value, moral requirements, and knowledge of them. It is also likely that there will be some differences in the content of their moral views even if there is also a great deal of overlap. Nevertheless, that need not so alienate theists and atheists from each other that they cannot, in very substantial ways, share a common moral world and a common moral understanding. Theistic and secular morality need not be fundamentally different in substance, while their accounts of the basis of moral value and moral obligation will differ profoundly.

There is an additional feature that distinguishes religious morality from secular morality. This is the role of grace. Not only is the ground of value non-natural, there is also the non-natural *agency* of God. It is through God's grace that there is revelation, and through grace the gift of salvation is possible. A religious morality is not simply a morality that makes room for God. Rather, it has a distinct structure and character, involving value and agency that transcend nature and human understanding. In addition, that there should be cosmic justice and redemption is a crucial element of theistic morality. That there is a real moral order, giving a point and gravity to virtue and vice, and providing a justification for suffering and evil (whether or not that justification is clear to us), is central to religious morality. The world is an order that is governed by a perfect and benevolent intelligence. It is for that reason that what we do is of real and lasting significance and amounts to more than just episodes of natural history. Our actions matter as part of a cosmic drama in which we participate. The theist typically does not conceive his position as "morality plus God." Rather, the view is that morality is incomplete and moral considerations lack authority unless they have a theistic basis. It could not be the case that morality is naturalistic, for naturalism cannot explain cosmic justice or redemption, and the moral order is incomplete without them.

An additional question concerns the motive to be moral. The critic of theism may wonder what is the importance of theism to morality if: (a) fundamental elements of morality are accessible to us without revelation; and (b) people can be motivated to act morally independent of considerations of divine command and eternal reward and punishment. Suppose a person does not believe that moral requirements are divine commands and does not believe that his or her life is a part of a providential plan for the world. How, if at all, is that agent disabled for moral motivation? Perhaps the agent is not disabled. This is one reason why critics of theistic morality regard theism as (at best) not necessary for morality. They argue that there is nothing essential to moral motivation that cannot be secured without God. Maybe some agents regard belief in God as essential to moral concern and moral resolve, but that should be interpreted as a psychological fact about those agents, not a discovery about morality. We can love our fellow man and strive to be just without believing in God or believing that the reasons to be just and to love our fellow man depend upon God. Here we shall just point out these basic questions regarding the relation of theism to both the status and authority of moral requirements, on the one hand, and the nature of moral motivation, on the other. You should consider in what ways, if any, theism makes an essential difference to the character of moral motivation and the nature of moral commitment. Apart from concerns about reward and punishment, how might the existence of God be crucial to understanding moral motivation?

Finally, it might seem that religious morality is a kind of subjectivism or relativism because of the fundamental role of faith in religion and because there are so many different faith-traditions. While there is a great deal of disagreement about matters of religion and the disagreements are not resolvable by rational demonstration, it is important to see that theists often understand their view as objectivist and realist. The fact that theism involves supernaturalism and a role for faith need not undercut the objectivity of God's commands. In addition, the theist might argue that the existence of God and the authority of divine command are the most solid certainties and are necessary bases for morality even if it is acknowledged that these are not matters of rational proof. That does not prove that the theist is right, but it is a reminder that just because there is a role for faith in religious morality, it is not necessarily also a kind of relativism or subjectivism. Faith may be the way in which we know important truths that are not accessible through empirical evidence or *a priori* reasoning.

There are, of course, many different religious traditions and many different ways of understanding religious faith, belief, and commitment. Still, it is not inevitable that differences between faiths and traditions should so divide people that moral consensus is rendered impossible or inherently unstable, at least in ways that are peculiarly severe just because of theism. Theists need not be hopelessly divided from each other any more than theists and atheists need to be. There are plenty of other things that divide people. Sometimes those divisions are seriously aggravated by religious differences, and sometimes faith brings people together, even when their faiths are different. Different religious traditions often share fundamental values and different faiths may share many basic moral convictions and concerns. The key issue for us here is whether theism is necessary for the genuineness of morality.

In sum, a very wide range of philosophical issues and positions is discernible in the debate about whether moral value is to be interpreted naturalistically. In addressing these questions positions as diverse as Platonism, emotivism, and theism are relevant. It is a topic with semantic, metaphysical, and epistemological dimensions – all of equal and interrelated importance.

Where Now?

With the conceptual tools and strategies of argument now at your command, you should be able to work your way more deeply into the philosophical dimensions of moral theorizing. You should also be able to see the ways in which even very different moral theories are attempts to address issues that are shared by all of them. The topics we have discussed, the distinctions we have formulated, and the positions we have characterized will be relevant to any further study of moral theory. Their significance is not confined to the thinkers referred to in this book. All of the debates that we identified remain very much alive and at the center of moral theorizing, and it is likely that they will remain so. There are certain inexhaustible questions that demand our best efforts of reflection and analysis, and when we engage them in a sustained, rigorous manner we are doing a good service to moral understanding by doing philosophy.

Questions for Discussion and Reflection

1 What are some of the main objections to a naturalistic interpretation of moral value? In what ways do those objections reflect considerations about the issue of moral motivation in particular?
2 What are the main features of the different interpretations of naturalism, and what are the main philosophical motivations for the different naturalistic accounts of moral value?
3 Moore focused on *good* as the fundamental moral concept. Other philosophers have regarded other concepts as fundamental; for example, *right* or *duty*. Consider one or more of those possibilities in light of Moore's understanding of the "naturalistic fallacy" and the "open question argument." How might those other values be defined (by someone who thought they could be)? What are the main results of the application of Moore's critical tools? Are they what Moore himself thought they were?
4 How should the relation between fact and value be understood? Is virtue-centered theorizing an effective strategy for formulating a naturalistic account of moral value?
5 How might an expressivist respond to the objection that expressivism (whether emotivist, prescriptivist, or in some other version) cannot adequately explain the way in which moral considerations make genuine claims upon us? Why might a critic think that this is a serious difficulty for expressivism?
6 Why might it be thought that theism is essential to morality, even while it is admitted that there may not be rational proof of the existence of God? What would be the loss to morality if it were non-theistic?

Thinkers and Their Works, and Further Reading

Thomas Aquinas: *Summa Theologica*
Aristotle: *Nicomachean Ethics*
A. J. Ayer: *Language, Truth and Logic*

Simon Blackburn: "Moral Realism"; "Errors and the Phenomenology of Value"

David Brink: *Moral Realism and the Foundations of Ethics*

Philippa Foot: "Moral Beliefs"; *Virtues and Vices*

Peter Geach: "The Moral Law and the Law of God"

Richard Hare: *The Language of Morals*; *Freedom and Reason*

Gilbert Harman: "Is There a Single True Morality?"; *The Nature of Morality*

David Hume: *An Enquiry Concerning the Principles of Morals*; *A Treatise of Human Nature*

Immanuel Kant: *Foundations of the Metaphysics of Morals*; *Critique of Practical Reason*

John McDowell: "Values and Secondary Qualities"; "Projection and Truth in Ethics"; "Two Sorts of Naturalism"

J. S. Mill: *Utilitarianism*

G. E. Moore: *Principia Ethica*

Plato: *Republic*

Peter Railton: "Moral Realism"

Nicholas Sturgeon: "Moral Explanations"; "Harman on Moral Explanations of Natural Facts"

Notes

1   G. E. Moore, *Principia Ethica* (Cambridge: Cambridge University Press, 1994), p. 58.
2   Ibid., p. 62.
3   Ibid., p. 58.
4   Ibid., p. 95.
5   J. S. Mill, *Utilitarianism* (Indianapolis: Hackett, 1979), p. 34.
6   Ibid., p. 38.
7   Moore, *Principia Ethica*, p. 67.
8   Ibid., p. 66.
9   Gilbert Harman, "Is There a Single True Morality," in *Morality, Reason and Truth*, ed. David Copp and David Zimmerman (Totowa, NJ: Rowman and Allanheld, 1985), p. 33.
10   David Brink, *Moral Realism and the Foundations of Ethics* (New York: Cambridge University Press, 1989), 160.
11   A. J. Ayer, *Language, Truth and Logic* (New York: Dover, 1952), p. 104.
12   Ibid., p. 107.
13   Ibid.

14 R. M. Hare, *Freedom and Reason* (Oxford: Oxford University Press, 1963), p. 4.

15 R. M. Hare, *The Language of Morals* (New York: Oxford University Press, 1964), p. 82.

16 Simon Blackburn, "Moral Realism," in *Essays in Quasi-realism* (New York: Oxford University Press, 1993), p. 122.

17 Hare, *The Language of Morals*, pp. 80–1.

18 David Hume, An *Enquiry Concerning the Principles of Morals*, 3rd edn, ed. L. A. Selby-Bigge (Oxford: Clarendon Press, 1975), p. 286.

19 Simon Blackburn, "Errors and the Phenomenology of Value," in *Essays in Quasi-realism* (New York: Oxford University Press, 1993), p. 157.

20 Philippa Foot, "Moral Beliefs," in *Virtues and Vices* (Berkeley: University of California Press, 1978), p. 112.

21 Ibid., p. 112-113.

22 John McDowell, "Values and Secondary Qualities," in *Essays on Moral Realism*, ed. Geoffrey Sayre-McCord (Ithaca, NY: Cornell University Press, 1988), p. 168.

23 Ibid.

24 Ibid., p. 176.

25 John McDowell, "Projection and Truth in Ethics," in *Moral Discourse and Practice*, ed. Stephen Darwall, Allan Gibbard, and Peter Railton (New York: Oxford University Press, 1997), p. 220.

26 Aristotle, *Nicomachean Ethics*, trans. Terence Irwin (Indianapolis: Hackett, 1985), 1104b, 14–15.

27 Ibid., 1140b, 5.

28 Ibid., 1141b, 13–14.

29 Ibid., 1144a, 10.

30 Skepticism about there being a best kind of life for a human being is a theme of a great deal of contemporary moral theorizing. Part of what motivates it is abandonment of the view that there is a normative world order or that there are natural purposes. The point is not that "nothing matters" but that the way in which things matter depends upon human concern and interest. If there are virtues that it is good for human beings to have it is not because exercise of them enables people to successfully actualize their nature, but because we can best attain our aspirations and pursue our interests by being certain sorts of people. That we should be those sorts of people, or that it is good to be like that, is not something that is objectively grounded in a common human nature, which it is our project to actualize or perfect in order to flourish as human beings. There are many different kinds of human flourishing and many different virtues, and they do not each have a specific place in one, privileged, best kind of life.

31 Gilbert Harman, *The Nature of Morality* (New York: Oxford University

Press, 1977), p. 7.

32   Ibid., p. 7.

33   Nicholas Sturgeon, "Moral Explanations," in *Essays on Moral Realism*, ed. Geoffrey Sayre-McCord (Ithaca, NY: Cornell University Press, 1988), p. 250.

34   Ibid., p. 250.

35   Peter Railton, "Moral Realism," in *Moral Discourse and Practice*, ed. Stephen Darwall, Allan Gibbard and Peter Railton (New York: Oxford University Press, 1997), p. 147.

36   Ibid., p. 155.

37   Plato, *Euthyphro*, trans. G. M. A. Grube (Indianapolis: Hackett, 1981), 10a, 14.

38   Immanuel Kant, *Foundations of the Metaphysics of Morals* (Indianapolis, Hackett Bobbs-Merrill, 1976), p. 25.

39   Thomas Aquinas, *Summa Theologica*, excerpted in *Introduction to Saint Thomas Aquinas*, ed. Anton C. Pegis (New York: Modern Library, 1948), Q. 90, Art. 4, p. 615.

40   Ibid.

41   Ibid., Q. 91, Art. 2, p. 618.

42   A view of this kind is defended by Peter Geach. See "The Moral Law and the Law of God" in *God and the Soul* (London: Routledge & Kegan Paul, 1969).

Conclusion

Too often, arguments about moral issues end in heated disagreement without many steps in reasoning being taken. Sometimes, we may not even realize that there are steps to take, instead of just digging in and rejecting views that oppose our own. Conceptual fluency and competence with the abstract issues can enable us to take more steps and to bring the issues more clearly into view. They also help us to notice the ways in which various aspects of an issue are related to each other. Overall, we are able to achieve a more subtle and multidimensional understanding. Many of the most interesting and contentious issues belong to metaethics and moral psychology. The better our understanding of those dimensions of moral issues, the higher the resolution we will achieve in looking at concrete problems. For example, there is nothing contrived about addressing the issue of pornography in terms of arguments about the nature of moral value, moral motivation, the place of moral considerations in our lives, and the relation between pleasure and moral value. It is a concrete, practical problem, but like many others (capital punishment, drug use, euthanasia, affirmative action, the rules of war, etc.) the more texture, rigor, and depth we bring to the consideration of it, the better able we will be to cogently develop and articulate a view of it.

Press any moral position firmly enough, and you will make contact with the metaethics and the moral psychology it presupposes or needs, and wherever you press will also exert pressure on other issues. This does not mean that there are straightforward implications from metaethical positions to specific moral positions. For instance, there are consequentialist and non-consequentialist theories that hold that value is objective. Similarly, many different moral theories could each be naturalistic. Different contract theorists arrive at quite different results. There is not a strict correlation between metaethics and moral psychology on the one hand and normative theory on the other, but we are better able to examine and evaluate the justification and coherence of a moral theory the more we understand its metaethical and moral psychological dimensions. If commitments concerning the nature and status of moral value, the character of moral agents, and moral motivation are suspect, implausible, or incompatible, that has a serious impact on the cogency and tenability of the moral theory.

Thinking about metaethics and moral psychology is also helpful in another regard. The philosophical architecture of moral theorizing shares a great deal of basic structure with other important philosophical issues. We noted analogies between some of the issues discussed here and the free will debate, and debates about perceptual knowledge. As we have noted, many of the questions we discussed are problems of philosophy in general, taking on certain distinctive forms in the context of moral theorizing. For example, there are controversies in metaphysics and the philosophy of science about whether the world order – what there is, and what it is like – is dependent upon our conceptual choices and descriptions, or has a standing in its own right independent of them. Along very similar lines, a key metaethical question is whether value is objective in a way that is independent of our desires, preferences, and beliefs.

There is also a debate about the status of laws of nature. Are the causal relations and relations of necessitation that are expressed by statements of laws to be interpreted realistically (as describing real features of the way the world works) or in terms of epistemological and pragmatic considerations, such as how we use certain kinds of statements in predictions and explanations? Some of the general features of that issue should be recognizable to you from our discussions of whether rightness and obligatoriness are objective features of the world, or grounded in attitudes, feelings, or stances. The question of whether moral value supervenes on non-moral facts and properties is not so different from the issue of whether epistemic justification supervenes on non-epistemic facts (e.g. facts about conditions of observation, our mental capacities and processes, and what is going on in the world). We say that some beliefs and knowledge claims are justified *because* . . . and then we fill in the "because" clause. That project is comparable in many ways to the task of filling in the "because" clause when we make claims about why an action is wrong or is a moral duty, and so forth. Moral philosophy clearly has its own special concerns and issues, but they have general features that are shared by other philosophical problems.

Exploring the dimensions of moral theory that we have discussed makes the study of moral theory both deeper and wider. It is made deeper by digging down to the presuppositions and assumptions that support it and give it much of its overall shape. It is made wider by bringing into relief affinities with other areas of philosophy. Noticing analogies, seeing how a concern in one context has counterparts in others, and realizing that the language of inquiry and analysis in one problem-area may have application in other contexts, brings things into much clearer view and enables us to make philosophical moves more effectively.

In the context of moral theorizing, as elsewhere in philosophy, it is important to avoid looking at the various positions as fixed options. They are not finished products from which we make a selection in order to please ourselves. One does not just decide to be a Platonist, or a Kantian, or an expressivist. Rather, we find ourselves endorsing certain theses and views of the issues on the basis of careful, sustained reasoning and reflection. Moreover, in theorizing about morality and in the examination of the theories themselves, the task of illuminating, explaining, and justifying is never complete or closed to further development. There are always new cases, questions, and challenges to any theory's coherence, scope, and plausibility. A theory is not a place to stop, to dig in, and rest one's case. It is a resource for grappling with issues that are always with us, and will always interest us, if we appreciate their depth and their significance to us as creatures capable of morality and philosophical reflection upon it.

Glossary

This is a glossary of terms used in this book. It is not intended to be a complete glossary of terms used in metaethics and moral psychology. For many of the entries, there are ongoing philosophical debates about how they are to be defined. Also, many of these terms have more than one sense. The definitions provided here are meant to be minimally controversial, and only the senses especially relevant to the discussions in the book are presented. At the end of several of the entries I have indicated names of thinkers who are especially important with regard to them.

antirealism: Antirealism in respect of some issue or subject matter denies that certain objects or properties exist. (For example, objective moral values, or causal relations between events.) We did not use the term in this book, but we did refer to Plato, Moore, and others as realists. (*See* realism.) (Ayer, Hare, Blackburn)

a priori: A knowledge claim is *a priori* if it is known to be true independent of sense experience and empirical information. Kant held that our knowledge of the moral law is *a priori*.

categorical imperative: In Kant's moral philosophy the categorical imperative is the fundamental law of morality. He offers several formulations of it, the first of which is "Act only according to that maxim by which you can at the same time will that it should become a universal law." He argued that moral duties are categorically (that is, unconditionally) imperative. Non-moral imperatives (e.g. "If you want to repair your car yourself, you ought to get a repair manual and a tool set") are hypothetically imperative. They indicate what is rationally required on some condition, such as having a certain desire or interest. Many moral theorists hold that moral imperatives are categorical, but Kant's use of the notion and his formulation of *the* categorical imperative as the fundamental moral law is the most widely known.

cognitivism: This is the view that moral statements (e.g. "murder is wrong," "each person has a duty to treat others fairly") are literally true or false. It is appropriate to evaluate them for truth or falsity, rather than taking them to be expressions of feelings or attitudes. (Plato, Aristotle, Mill, Kant, Moore, Foot, McDowell)

consequentialism: A moral theory is a consequentialist theory if it holds that the moral value of actions is to be found in what they bring about, or the states of affairs they cause. The morality of an act is determined by its consequences (or intended consequences) rather than, say, the agent's motive or the agent's character. The moral value of an action is not intrinsic to it. (Mill, Moore)

constructivism: This is a type of cognitivism in which moral facts or principles are constructions of moral thought, rather than discovered or detected, as in the realist view. (Kant, Rawls)

contractarian theory: The contract approach to moral theory is a strategy for ascertaining moral principles on the basis of a conception of what rational agents would agree to, or what agents would rationally accept as binding. Agents are conceived of as fashioning the basic terms of agreement for entry into a civil society governed by norms all can accept. Rights and obligations depend upon the content of the contract and are not prior to it. (*See* original position.) (Rawls, Gauthier, Hobbes, Locke, Scanlon)

deontological: A moral theory is a deontological theory if it takes the notion of a right action, or an agent's rights and duties, to be basic, in contrast to what is basic in a consequentialist or virtue-centered theory. (Kant, Ross)

egoism: Psychological egoism is the thesis that people always and only act with a view toward their own (perceived) self-interest – they never act in a genuinely altruistic or disinterested way. Ethical egoism is the position that people ought to act always and only with a view toward their own self-interest, and that they should not be motivated by considerations of altruism. (Hobbes)

emotivism: This is a type of expressivism. Early twentieth-century expressivist theories were versions of emotivism, with an emphasis on the non-cognitive character of moral claims. They do not report facts.

Moral language has emotive or expressive meaning but not cognitive meaning. (*See* prescriptivism.) (Ayer)

error theory: A theory of moral judgment is an error theory when it holds that at least some fundamental assumptions of ordinary moral discourse are in fact false. J. L. Mackie interpreted moral discourse on the basis of what he called an "error theory," claiming that the use of moral language presupposes that there are objective values, but upon philosophical examination, we find that there are none. Thus, ordinary moral discourse is based on an error, a systematic misconception of its basis. It is not meaningless, but it is false.

expressivism: This is the view that moral judgments are expressive rather than assertions of moral facts or beliefs. Moral judgments express feelings, attitudes, or stances and are not literally true or false. It is often part of expressivist views that moral language is used not only to express feelings and so forth, but also to influence others. This view is opposed to cognitivism. (Ayer, Hare, Blackburn)

hedonism: This is a theory of value according to which pleasure is the good. Pleasure is what is ultimately desired for its own sake, and therefore, it is what it is rational to pursue and maximize. (Mill)

intuitionism: This is an epistemological notion, and it is used in two ways in moral theorizing. According to one usage, a moral intuitionist argues that we have noninferential, direct knowledge of (*prima facie*) moral duties. W. D. Ross is an intuitionist in that sense. In the other sense, the one in which Moore was an intuitionist, we have intuitive knowledge of good, but we do not have intuitive knowledge of moral duties. (*See prima facie.*)

monism: This is the view that there is one fundamental moral value. For example, Mill held that all questions of moral value are ultimately questions of utility. Kant argued that moral worth is to be found solely in volitions that respect the moral law and thereby respect rational agency (one's own, and that of other agents). (*See* pluralism.) (Mill, Kant)

naturalism: There are many different interpretations of moral naturalism, but the basic, common idea of moral naturalism is that moral value can be understood in terms of the kinds of properties and facts that can be described by common sense and the sciences. Moral value is not something outside of nature. Many naturalists argue that moral value supervenes on natural properties. (*See* supervenience.) (Mill, Aristotle, Sturgeon, Railton)

non-cognitivism: This is the denial of cognitivism. Moral claims are not literally true or false. They are meaningful, but have expressive meaning, and do not moral state facts. (Ayer, Hare, Blackburn)

non-consequentialism: A moral theory is a non-consequentialist theory if it holds that the moral value of an action is intrinsic to it, and determined by the motive of the agent, the agent's character, or the principle on which the agent acted, in contrast to the consequences (or intended consequences) of the act.

non-naturalism: This is the view that moral value is distinct from, and cannot be exhaustively explained in terms of, natural properties and facts. (Moore, Kant, Plato)

objective: The fundamental claim of objectivists is that moral judgments are cognitive judgments. Many objectivists also hold that moral values and moral reasons are independent of desires, beliefs, and attitudes. Some objectivists hold that moral value is an entity or property, which is a reality independent of minds. (Plato, Kant, Moore, Ross, Aristotle, Mill)

original position: In John Rawls's contract theory, the original position of parties to the contract is such that they do not know what their positions will be in the resulting society. They have general knowledge of human nature, but do not know their own particular abilities, advantages, or disadvantages, and so forth. The original position is a theoretical device for ensuring that the contract is fair, because there is no scope for parties to exploit advantages in ability or position. (Rawls)

perfectionism: A perfectionist moral theory bases moral requirements on a view of how an individual can most completely and properly develop his capacities — how the agent can most fully approximate to an ideal of human nature or rational agency. (Aristotle)

pluralism: This is the view that there is more than one fundamental moral value or principle. For example, a theory may recognize autonomy, welfare, and rights as having fundamental value, and these are not reducible to one value or source of value. (*See* monism.) (Aristotle, Ross, Nagel)

prescriptivism: This is a type of expressivism. It emphasizes universalization as a feature of moral claims, and treats them as having the form of commands, as prescribing certain behavior, based upon the attitude or stance of the person making the claim. (Hare)

prima facie: W. D. Ross argued that we have intuitive knowledge of *prima facie* duties. That is, we recognize some moral duties are basic and uninferred, in virtue of certain features of a situation. For example, there is a *prima facie* duty to keep one's promises. When all of the morally relevant features of a situation are considered, the *prima facie* duty may yield to a judgment of what is required, all things considered. But what is *prima facie* obligatory is always morally relevant. (*See* intuitionism.)

realism: Realism with regard to some issue or subject matter asserts that certain objects or properties exist (for example, objective moral values, or causal relations between events). (Plato, Aristotle, Nagel, Moore, Mill, Sturgeon, Railton)

relativism: Moral relativism denies moral realism and is also the view that moral value and the correctness of moral judgments are always relative to the norms, perspectives, or conventions of different subjects. These may be cultures, societies, historical periods, or other specifications of groups, or even individuals, to which moral values or judgments are relative.

skepticism: There are different versions of moral skepticism. The moral skeptic may be denying that there are objective moral values, or that any moral claims are true. Or, the moral skeptic might take the more radical position that there are no moral values at all. Skepticism is an important position in all areas of philosophy, and in general the skeptic denies that there is knowledge or justified belief with respect to some subject matter or area of dispute (perceptual knowledge, for example). (Mackie)

subjective: The main elements of subjectivism are that moral value has its ground or source in human feelings, desires, or beliefs, and that moral judgments are not cognitive judgments.

supervenience: A property supervenes on another property or group of properties when the latter, the underlying or base properties, determine the former, the supervening property. The latter cannot be present without the base properties, and wherever they are found, it is found, though the supervening property cannot be reduced to the base properties. Many theorists hold that moral properties supervene on natural properties. (*See* naturalism.) (Sturgeon, Railton)

teleology: Teleology concerns ends or purposes. Aristotle's theory of virtues is teleological in that it is based upon a conception of what is the proper end for human nature. Virtuous activity enables the agent to fully actualize or realize his or her nature, and that activity is also pleasing. There are objective goods that are proper to human nature, given its distinctive capacities. The virtuous agent has a correct conception of those goods, and activity guided by that conception is the cause of the agent leading a flourishing life. (Aristotle)

utilitarianism: This is a type of consequentialism. In its most influential version, it holds that the morally relevant feature of an action is the extent to which it brings about an increase in pleasure, welfare, or happiness, or a reduction in pain. However, it is possible to be a utilitarian without also holding a hedonist theory of value. (Mill, Moore [a non-hedonist utilitarian])

virtue-centered theory: A virtue-centered theory maintains that moral value is grounded in certain excellent states of character (the virtues) and that actions have moral worth through being exercises of those states of character. Virtue-centered theories (such as Aristotle's) often include the claim that there is a best overall kind of life for a human being, which is achieved through the integrated, harmonious exercise of the virtues. Excellent activity is naturally pleasing in this view. (Aristotle, Plato)

Bibliography

Aquinas, Thomas (1948) *Summa Theologica*, excerpted in *Introduction to Saint Thomas Aquinas*, edited by Anton C. Pegis. New York: The Modern Library.

Aristotle (1985) *Nicomachean Ethics*, translated by Terence Irwin. Indianapolis: Hackett Publishing Company.

Ayer, A. J. (1952) *Language, Truth and Logic*. New York: Dover Publications.

Blackburn, Simon (1993) "Errors and the Phenomenology of Value." In *Essays in Quasi-realism*. New York: Oxford University Press.

Blackburn, Simon (1993) "How to Be an Ethical Antirealist." In *Essays in Quasi-realism*. New York: Oxford University Press.

Blackburn, Simon (1993) "Moral Realism." In *Essays in Quasi-realism*. New York: Oxford University Press.

Brink, David (1989) *Moral Realism and the Foundations of Ethics*. New York: Cambridge University Press.

Chisholm, Roderick (1957) *Perceiving: A Philosophical Study*. Ithaca, NY: Cornell University Press.

Chisholm, Roderick (1989) *Theory of Knowledge*, 3rd edn. New York: Prentice Hall.

Foot, Philippa (1978) "Moral Beliefs." In *Virtues and Vices*. Berkeley: University of California Press.

Gauthier, David (1985) "Justice as Social Choice." In *Morality, Reason and Truth*, edited by David Copp and David Zimmerman. Totowa, NJ: Rowman and Allanheld.

Gauthier, David (1987) *Morals by Agreement*. Oxford: Oxford University Press.

Geach, Peter (1969) "The Moral Law and the Law of God." In *God and the Soul*. London: Routledge and Kegan Paul.

Hare, Richard (1963) *Freedom and Reason*. Oxford: Oxford University Press.

Hare, Richard (1973) *The Language of Morals*. New York: Oxford University

Press.

Harman, Gilbert (1977) *The Nature of Morality*. New York: Oxford University Press.

Harman, Gilbert (1985) "Is There a Single True Morality?" In *Morality, Reason and Truth*, edited by David Copp and David Zimmerman. Totowa, NJ: Rowman and Allenheld.

Hume, David (1975) *An Enquiry Concerning the Principles of Morals*, edited by L. A. Selby-Bigge. Oxford: Clarendon Press.

Hume, David (1978) *A Treatise of Human Nature*, edited by L. A. Selby-Bigge. Oxford: Oxford University Press.

Hursthouse, Rosalind (1998) "Applying Virtue Ethics." In *Virtues and Reasons*, edited by Rosalind Hurtshouse, Gavin Lawrence, and Warren Quinn. Oxford: Clarendon Press.

Kant, Immanuel (1960) *Religion within the Limits of Reason Alone*, edited by Theodore M. Greene and Hoyt H. Hudson. New York: Harper & Row.

Kant, Immanuel (1964) *The Doctrine of Virtue*, translated by Mary J. Gregor. Philadelphia: University of Pennsylvania Press.

Kant, Immanuel (1976). *Foundations of the Metaphysics of Morals*. Indianapolis: Bobbs-Merrill.

Kant, Immanuel (1993) *Critique of Practical Reason*, translated by L. W. Beck. New York: Macmillan.

Korsgaard, Christine (1986) "Skepticism about Practical Reason." *Journal of Philosophy*, 83(1), 5–25.

Korsgaard, Christine (1997) *The Sources of Normativity*. Cambridge: Cambridge University Press.

Locke, John (1988) *Two Treatises of Government*, edited by P. Laslett. Cambridge: Cambridge University Press.

Mackie, John (1977) *Ethics: Inventing Right and Wrong*. Harmondsworth: Penguin.

McDowell, John (1978) "Are Moral Requirements Hypothetical Imperatives?" In *Proceedings of the Aristotelian Society*, supplementary volume 52.

McDowell, John (1979) "Virtue and Reason." *Monist*, 62, 331–50.

McDowell, John (1988) "Values and Secondary Qualities." In *Essays on Moral Realism*, edited by Geoffrey Sayre-McCord. Ithaca, NY: Cornell University Press.

McDowell, John (1997) "Projection and Truth in Ethics." In *Moral Discourse and Practice*, edited by Stephen Darwall, Allan Gibbard, and Peter Railton. New York: Oxford University Press.

McDowell, John (1998) "Two Sorts of Naturalism." In *Virtues and Reasons*, edited by Rosalind Hursthouse, Gavin Lawrence, and Warren Quinn. Oxford: Clarendon Press.

McNaughton, David (2000) "Intuitionism." In *The Blackwell Guide to Ethical Theory*, edited by Hugh LaFollette. Oxford: Blackwell.

Mill, J. S. (1979) *Utilitarianism*. Indianapolis: Hackett Publishing Company.

Moore, G. E. (1994) *Principia Ethica*. Cambridge: Cambridge University Press.

Nagel, Thomas (1970) *The Possibility of Altruism*. Princeton, NJ: Princeton University Press.

Nagel, Thomas (1985) "The Fragmentation of Value." In *Mortal Questions*. New York: Cambridge University Press.

Nagel, Thomas (1986) *The View from Nowhere*. New York: Oxford University Press.

Plato (1981) *Euthyphro*. In *Five Dialogues*, translated by G. M. A. Grube. Indianapolis: Hackett Publishing Company.

Plato (1992) *Republic*, translated by G. M. A. Grube. Indianapolis: Hackett Publishing Company.

Plato (1997) *Plato: Complete Works*, edited by J. M. Cooper and D. S. Hutchinson. Indianapolis: Hackett Publishing Company.

Railton, Peter (1997) "Moral Realism." In *Moral Discourse and Practice*, edited by Stephen Darwall, Allan Gibbard, and Peter Railton. New York: Oxford University Press.

Rawls, John (1971) *A Theory of Justice*. Cambridge, MA: Harvard University Press.

Rawls, John (1997) "Kantian Constructivism in Moral Theory." In *Moral Discourse and Practice*, edited by Stephen Darwall, Allan Gibbard, and Peter Railton. New York: Oxford University Press.

Reid, Thomas (1983) *Essays on the Active Powers*, excerpted in *Inquiry and Essays*, edited by Ronald E. Beanblossom and Keith Lehrer. Indianapolis: Hackett Publishing Company.

Ross, W. D. (1930) *The Right and the Good*. Oxford: Clarendon Press.

Scanlon, Thomas (1997) "Contractualism and Utilitarianism." In *Moral Discourse and Practice*, edited by Stephen Darwall, Allan Gibbard, and Peter Railton. New York: Oxford University Press.

Scanlon, Thomas (1998) *What We Owe to Each Other*. Cambridge, MA: Belknap Press.

Smart, J. J. C. and Williams, B. A. O. (1973) *Utilitarianism: For and Against*. Cambridge: Cambridge University Press.

Smith, Adam (1984) *The Theory of Moral Sentiments*, edited by D. D. Raphael and A. L. MacFie. Indianapolis: Liberty Fund.

Sturgeon, Nicholas (1986) "Harman on Moral Explanations of Natural Facts." *Southern Journal of Philosophy*, supplementary volume 14, 69–78.

Sturgeon, Nicholas (1988) "Moral Explanations." In *Essays on Moral Realism*, edited by Geoffrey Sayre-McCord. Ithaca, NY: Cornell University Press.

Williams, Bernard (1981) "Moral Luck." In *Moral Luck*. New York: Cambridge.

Williams, Bernard (1981) "Persons, Character and Morality." In *Moral Luck*. New York: Cambridge University Press.

Williams, Bernard (1985) *Ethics and the Limits of Philosophy*. Cambridge, MA: Harvard University Press.

Wittgenstein, Ludwig (1972) *On Certainty*, edited by G. E. M. Anscombe. New York: HarperCollins.

Wolf, Susan (1982) "Moral Saints." *Journal of Philosophy*, 79(8), 419–39.

Index

32326401R00109

Made in the USA
San Bernardino, CA
02 April 2016

To: Jack Capra
thank you for
supporting our
Masonic Home.

Interpreting Masonic Ritual

Oscar Patterson III

Fraternally
W: Oscar Patterson

Hamilton Books

An Imprint of
Rowman & Littlefield
Lanham • Boulder • New York • Toronto • Plymouth, UK

Copyright © 2017 by Hamilton Books
4501 Forbes Boulevard, Suite 200, Lanham, Maryland 20706
Hamilton Books Acquisitions Department (301) 459-3366

Unit A, Whitacre Mews, 26-34 Stannary Street,
London SE11 4AB, United Kingdom

Library of Congress Control Number: 2016953957
ISBN: 978-0-7618-6860-6 (pbk : alk. paper)—ISBN: 978-0-7618-6861-3 (electronic)

♾™ The paper used in this publication meets the minimum requirements of American National Standard for Information Sciences Permanence of Paper for Printed Library Materials, ANSI/NISO Z39.48-1992.

To my Father

A Freemason

His true deeds were his secrets